THE FORGOTTEN AMERICAN VOLUNTEER GROUP

US Volunteers in the Colombia-Peru War, 1932

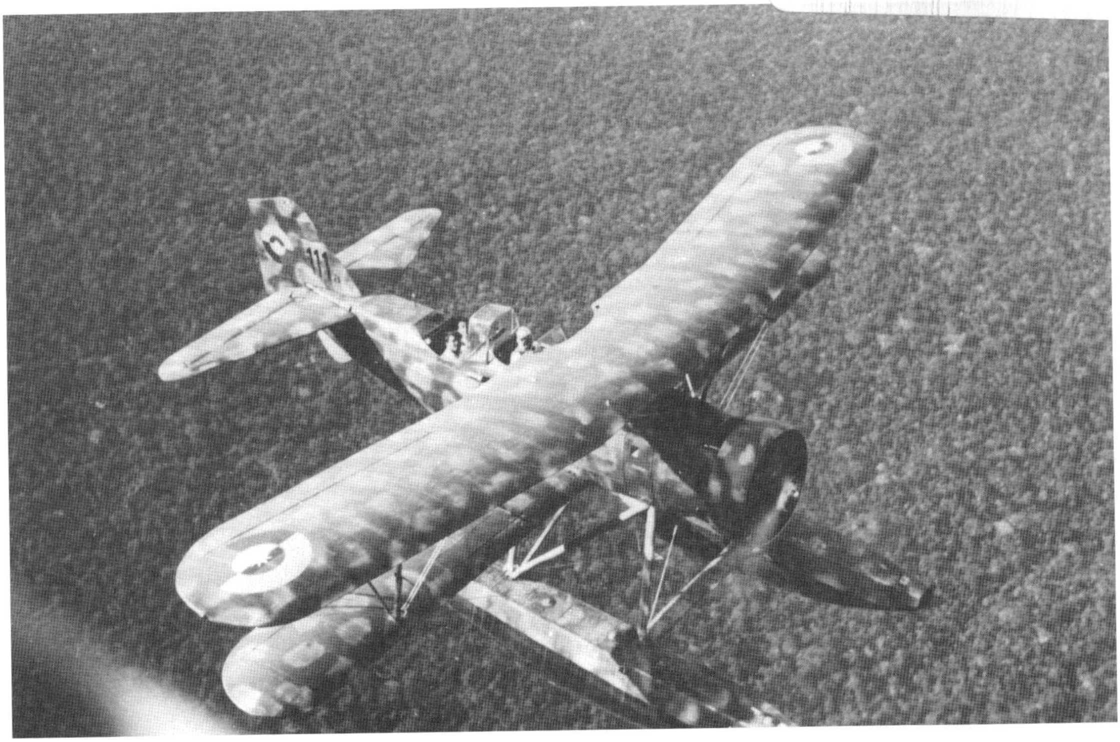

DAN HAGEDORN

KEY Books

Published by Key Books
An imprint of Key Publishing Ltd
PO Box 100
Stamford
Lincs PE19 1XQ

www.keypublishing.com

The right of Dan Hagedorn to be identified as the author of this book has been asserted in accordance with the Copyright, Designs and Patents Act 1988 Sections 77 and 78.

Copyright © Dan Hagedorn, 2020

ISBN 978 1 913870 02 7

All rights reserved. Reproduction in whole or in part in any form whatsoever or by any means is strictly prohibited without the prior permission of the Publisher.

Typeset by SJmagic DESIGN SERVICES, India.

Contents

Chapter 1	Introduction	4
	The Putumayo – Key to the Campaign	6
Chapter 2	The *Aviación Militar* at the Dawn of the 1930s	7
	Colombia Seeks an Amphibious Aircraft	8
	Those Curtiss Fledgling J-2s	9
	But What About *Ricaurte*?	11
	The Potential Game Changer: Enter the Junkers Ju 52/3m	13
	Dramatic Growth	14
	And Then the Junkers K 43	15
Chapter 3	The Curtiss-Wright Connection	18
	German Agitation Against American Equipment	22
Chapter 4	Colombia Attacks	24
	The Reluctant Field Marshal?	28
	Meanwhile, in the Combat Zone…	29
Chapter 5	Curtiss-Wright Arrives in Force, Just as the Dust Settles	32
	More Trainers	34
	And Then the Falcons	34
	The *Aviación Militar* Struts its Stuff	40
	That Colombian Camouflage	42
	The *Aviación Militar* Serial Number System	44
Chapter 6	*El Misión de Aviación Norteamericana*	53
	More Aircraft Arrive	54
	Even More Aircraft Arrive	64
	Big Orders with Too Much Momentum	65
	Those Bellanca 77-140s	71
	And Last but Not Least, Those Severskys	74
Chapter 7	Flying in Colombia	77
Chapter 8	A Few Words About the Opposition	79
	Equipping the CAP	80
	The Air Pageant of September 23, 1932	81
Chapter 9	Opening Moves and the Combat Period	83
Epilogue		88
Endnotes		92

Chapter 1
Introduction

As the worldwide effects of the Great Depression of the late 1920s spread far and wide, even remote and unlikely places felt the impact, as local grievances and politics, fueled by economic forces, offered the opportunity for settling old scores. Our story has its roots in one such obscure locale and, in order to understand how the narrative unfolds, a bit of background is essential.

What follows is a *very* abbreviated summary of a convoluted series of events which may be more fully explored in *Latin American Air Wars and Aircraft, 1912–1969*, Chapter 13 (including the expanded, downloadable text still available via Crecy/Hikoki, 2005). What became known as the "Leticia Dispute," stated simply, arose over a Peruvian attempt to repudiate a valid treaty – and, to regain by violence, territory ceded to Colombia.

Referred to as "not the end of the earth, but you can see it from there," Leticia itself, at the southernmost side of what was known as the Leticia quadrilateral, was a small, neat little village of fewer than 150 souls on a low plateau in the midst of a vast, marshy jungle. It enjoyed no communication via surface road whatsoever with any other town in Colombia, although it was occasionally visited from southwestern Colombia, to the rejoicing of its citizens, by river steamboats motoring eastward on the Putumayo to the Amazon, about 150 miles below Leticia, and thence onward to civilization.

On September 1, 1932, about 300 Peruvians, usually described as "civilians" in dispatches, living in the Colombian Intendancy of the Amazonas, suddenly descended upon sleepy Leticia and imprisoned its intendant, one Alfredo Villamil Fajardo, together with his entire garrison of ten totally bewildered Colombian soldiers and a few administrative civilians, finally shoving them off across the border into Brazil, and then took possession of the wireless station there. The entire action was performed without bloodshed, during the early morning hours. It was unquestionably the most exciting thing that had ever happened there.

In Iquitos, the capital of the Peruvian Department of Loreto, also on the upper Amazon, about 250 miles upriver from Leticia, the citizens, somehow learning of this extraordinary event, paraded "spontaneously" in celebration of "…the rescue and reincorporation of the Peruvian territory of Leticia."

The news of this event did not reach Bogotá – and Lima – for four to five days, so remote was the entire affair. The government in Lima was, to put it bluntly, unsure what to make of all of this while, in Bogotá, the newspapers, always sensationalist, expressed what they described as the indignation and hurt of the Republic in their heartfelt patriotism. Within a matter of days, the action was being described as "treacherous, felonious and cunning," prompting patriotic marches through the streets of the Colombian capital by schoolchildren as young as six, led by their teachers and priests, who chanted, "*Sanchez Cerro morirá y Colombia vencerá*" ("Sanchez Cerro will die and Colombia will win"). There was a general clamor to go to war with Peru over this grievous slight to Colombian sovereignty.

Rumors ran rampant about what else the Peruvians were getting up to, but facts were in noticeably short supply, there being no practical means of communicating with the remote outpost once the Peruvians had seized the radio station there – the solitary means of contact with the outside world.

The truth was that, despite all the bluster, Colombia really had no significant economic interests at stake in Leticia – nor anywhere in the dismal territory surrounding it – and so it boiled down to

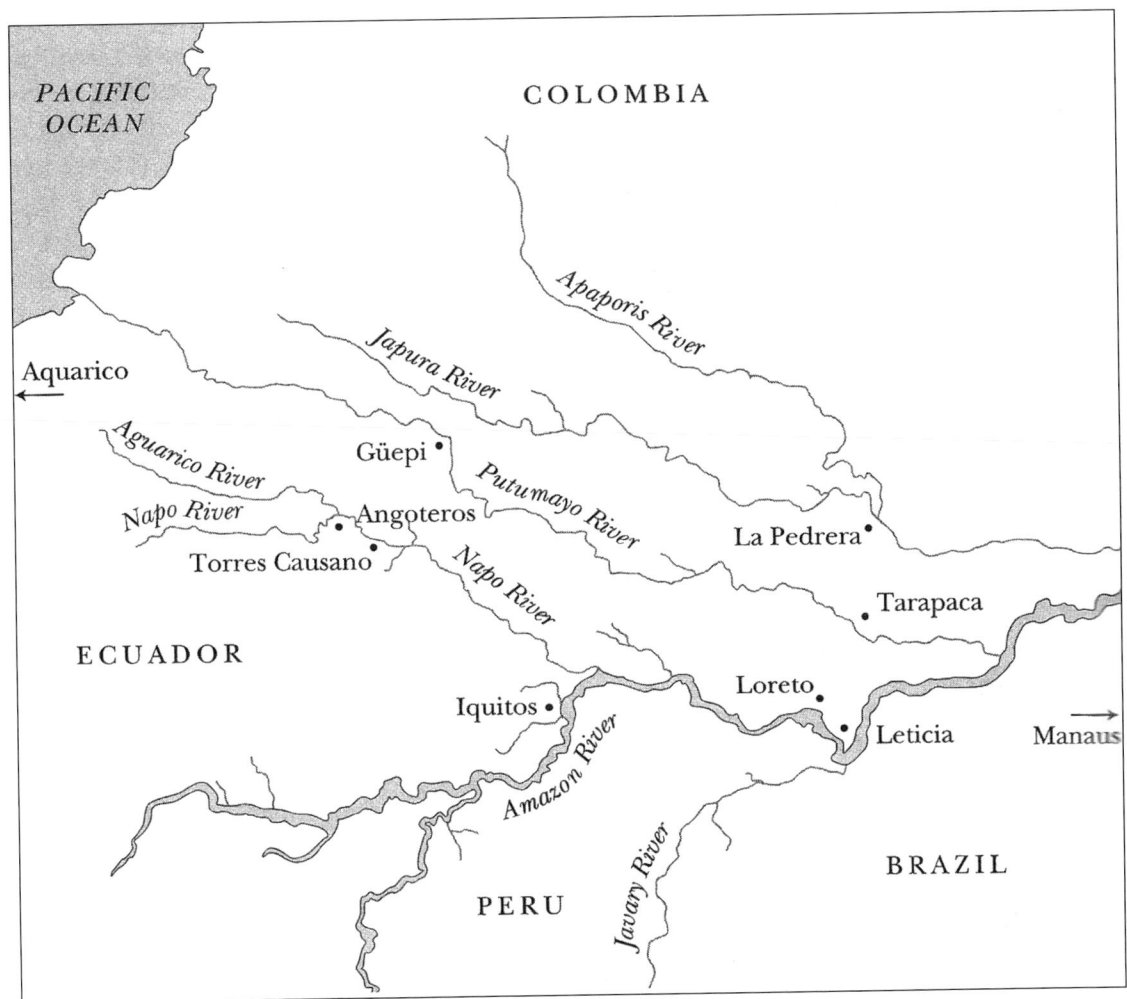

Maps do not do justice to the extremes of terrain that confronted the combatants in the Leticia region. Mountains, trackless jungle and swamp, and the network of tributaries that fed the mighty Amazon, made for what was, essentially, waterborne aviation assets. This map represents the general operating area.

national pride. Indeed, the only enterprises of any note there were a sugar plantation and lumber mill known as "La Victoria" which, significantly, was owned by a Peruvian, Dr. Enrique Vigil, who was, truth be known, the actual "Jefe" in the region.

The relatively small section of land between the Amazon and Putumayo rivers, usually cited colloquially as "the Colombian corridor," had been arbitrarily transferred to Colombia by Peru two years previously, to give the country an outlet on the upper Amazon.

The Peruvians still living there, probably the only people who really had a vested interest in the area, were determined to reincorporate the land into what they considered their country, Peru. So far as can be determined, no Colombian farmers or traders had actually settled there.

Indeed, according to the annual report of Father Gaspar, the Colombian Bishop of Cadossia, there were – in the entire disputed region – 188 houses (mostly humble huts), with a total population of 1,644, mostly native Ticuna Indians, nearly all of whom still spoke their own language. Of these, 56 of the dwellings were noted as being occupied by Spanish-descended Peruvians, ten by Brazilian citizens, and only two by Colombians – and then the five Colombian government officers, for whom Leticia must have been indeed a hardship assignment! There were also single dwellings occupied by Bolivian and Spanish nationals, who were truly a long way from home.

But more to the point, of the 1,644 people noted by the bishop, only 150 were actually living in Leticia proper. A U.S. consular officer, A. E. Milmore, had reportedly passed through Leticia several years prior to the emergency, and did not mince words when he described the poor town as "a group of about a score of poor shacks with a population of maybe 100 people. The whole region seemed to be an endless, swampy, mosquito-infested land of not much value."

Although Colombia had gained the "corridor" to the Amazon, the truth was that it still afforded Colombia no practical value, as any products grown in Colombia's eastern territories of the Caquetá and Putumayo could only be exported by shipping them down these rivers. Both disembogued into the Amazon in Brazilian territory – the Caquetá about 500 miles and the Putumayo about 200 miles below Leticia. Unfortunately, there were no such products being grown in those territories at the time.

The Colombian government was undoubtedly aware, at some level, of the actual state of affairs in Leticia, but nonetheless seized the opportunity presented by the surprise move there to arouse public sentiment to a high pitch of patriotism, and thereby gain support to float a National Defense Loan of about $9.5 million – a huge sum in 1932 during the deepest throes of the Depression. The President and his wife allegedly donated their wedding rings to this fund, which set off an orgy of such demonstrations throughout the Republic. One can only ponder the true fate of all of this jewelry.

And so, Colombia, and then Peru, commenced an arms race. A conventional war in that inhospitable region was virtually impossible, even with unlimited resources, and so, it was soon concluded, the entire matter would need to be resolved via rapid transformation of the nascent military aviation capabilities of the two nations, with modest riverine naval investment as well. To try to field even modest ground forces of, say, 5,000 to 10,000 men in the region would have quickly bankrupted both nations. The answer was, therefore, aviation.

The Putumayo – Key to the Campaign

In studying this bizarre conflict, students often focus entirely on the hardware and key actions, while ignoring the solitary factor which actually dictated everything else – the fact that the mighty Putumayo River was the solitary route for Colombia into the region, period. It was simply impossible to reach the region by land or through the jungles.

The actual border between Peru and Colombia was on the *right* bank of the river, and about halfway down was the modest Peruvian fort at Puerto Arturo, which had several artillery pieces. Clearly, the only way for Colombia to reach the disputed area was by going down the river "from the top." Aviation offered only slight variations, and the fact that Colombian aviators were instructed to keep the river in sight at all times limited even this additional dimension to that central geographic reality – and explains why nearly every aircraft that operated in the zone was either float-equipped or a seaplane.

Chapter 2
The *Aviación Militar* at the Dawn of the 1930s

The largely French-equipped Colombian national air arm of the 1920s had all but withered to next to nothing by 1926, when the organization was effectively placed in the hands of an aviation mission from, of all places, neutral Switzerland, replacing the last vestiges of the unfortunate French mission of 1921–24. Lasting only until July 31, 1928, the brief Swiss experiment was supplanted by yet another small French mission, in the person of Commandant Pierre Châteauvieux and a single engineer, M. Faure. Described locally as essentially a "family affair" (one of the members of the mission was said to be a relative of the French Minister to Colombia) this contract ended abruptly, too, in December 1931. His impact on the AM[1] was minimal, and only a single order for French aircraft was generated as a result of his tenure – ten Caudron C.59Et2 trainers around May 1928 – but this was abruptly cancelled when it was learned that his commission on the sale was regarded as, even by Colombian standards of the day, outrageous.

The primary benefit of these missions, which were numerous elsewhere in Latin America during the 1920s and 1930s, was the introduction into Colombia of 12 fairly modern, new-build aircraft, consisting of at least eight Wild-Comte X reconnaissance bomber biplanes (MSNs 5 to 12) mounting

The AM owed a considerable debt to the eight Wild-Comte X biplanes acquired from Switzerland in 1928, which helped prepare their cadre for what was to come. Sturdy and reliable, the surviving six were re-engined in 1933 as part of the Curtiss-Wright contract with 460hp Whirlwind engines.

420hp Gnome Rhone 9ADX Jupiter engines, which arrived starting May 6, 1928. These gained Colombian serials 101 to 108. The Model Xs actually followed three Wild WT43Ds (MSNs 1 to 3), with 185hp Hispano-Suiza engines, Colombian serials 11 to 14, which had arrived in 1927 and a single Wild WT, which was assembled in February 1925.

The small but energetic Swiss mission and the rejuvenated *Aviación Militar* (AM) worked their new mounts hard, and veteran Colombian airmen extolled the reliability and sturdiness of the aircraft. WT43D MSN 14, for example, made no fewer than 2,405 flights between delivery in 1927 and an accident on July 5, 1928, amassing 315:29 flight hours.

In truth, the renewed AM cadre owed much to the Swiss aircraft when the transition to what was to follow took place. By March 15, 1933, by which time conflict with Peru had developed, six of the Model Xs survived (although inactive) and, in a little-known effort to extend the service lives of these aircraft, Curtiss-Wright sent a mechanic to Colombia on March 17 with the specific task of re-engining the Wild Xs with 460hp Whirlwind engines. This work was apparently carried out, but oddly, little is known of any use of the newly re-engined aircraft in the conflict, and, as they were not able to be fitted with pontoons, it is assumed they were engaged as trainers.

Colombia Seeks an Amphibious Aircraft

The utility of water-based aircraft had been impressed upon the AM by the hugely successful SCADTA airline operations in the country, which had matured into one of the world's most effective airline operations by the end of the 1920s.

While the Swiss Wild-Comte aircraft had provided spartan service and had enabled the AM to "show the flag" throughout the country, they were unable to reach the remote stretches of the country, which were accessible only via the extensive river networks.

As a direct consequence, the AM sent one of its ablest officers, Mayor Benjamin Mendez Rey,[2] to the U.S. in early April 1931 to take delivery of four aircraft from the Curtiss-Wright Export Corporation. These consisted of three sturdy Fledgling trainers, which finally arrived in September – responding to what we would describe in current form as an "Urgent Operational Requirement," as the AM effectively

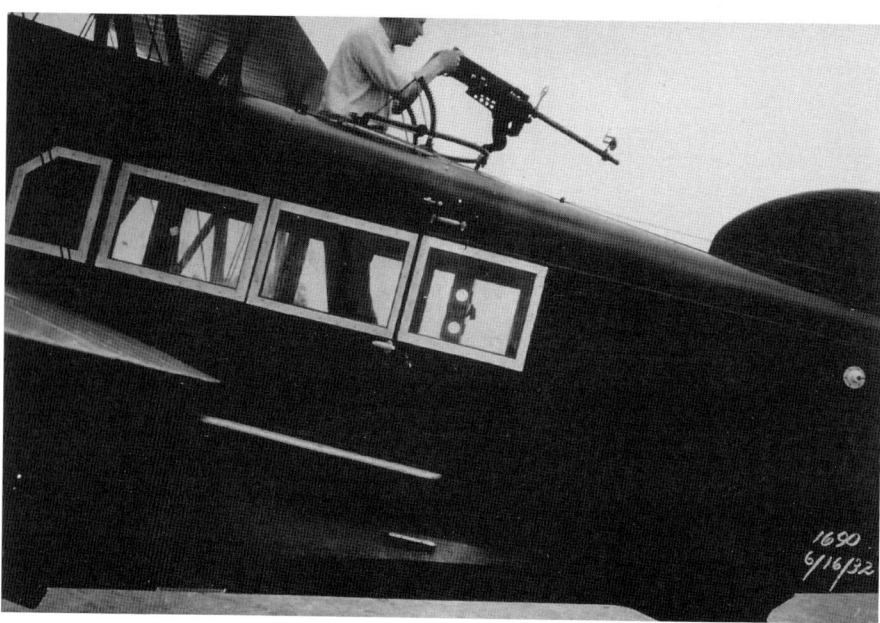

One of the first major acquisitions made by Colombia in her effort to equip her small air arm with aircraft capable of operating on the nation's extensive river systems was aborted. Rarely illustrated, this is the dorsal gun installation on one of the two Loening C-2CE amphibians ordered in 1931.

had no dedicated training aircraft or organization *per se*, although the Swiss aircraft had been rather casually engaged in this way briefly. These were the only variants of the Fledgling to be powered with a 240hp Wright engine.

The fourth aircraft on the order, however, is a bit of an enigma and is described as a hybrid "Keystone-Loening OL-8/OL-9 with a 410hp engine." Mendez found the aircraft to have been used and modified, as an obvious attraction to the Colombian delegation, to armed configuration from a purely civilian machine. Undaunted, the Colombians cancelled that portion of this first contract and, in March 1932, renewed their attempt to acquire amphibians by placing an order for two Loening C-2CEs equipped with a fixed .30-caliber gun in the port (left) upper wing, a flexible gun in a dorsal position, two A-3 bomb racks, 525hp R-1750 Cyclone engines, and fixtures for a single Fairchild K-3 camera, at a total cost of $45,000.

When Mendez traveled to the manufacturer in June 1932 to check on the progress on these aircraft, he once again discovered that one of the two aircraft had been used and, proclaiming deceit on the part of the Curtiss-Wright Export Corp., the Colombian government once again cancelled the order.

Thus, although Colombia clearly coveted the utility of the Loening design, and contrary to numerous reports, none actually reached the AM.[3]

Those Curtiss Fledgling J-2s

While Curtiss-Wright may well, in retrospect, be deserving of claims of profiteering and arms proliferation in the midst of struggling to survive the harshest depths of the worldwide Depression, the fact remains that the organization exercised a profound service to the evolution of Colombian aeronautics by laying out for the AM a plethora of state-of-the-art, capable aircraft to meet the needs of the service.

And so, between September 1931 and June 16, 1933, when a repeat order was placed, the AM contracted for – initially – six sturdy, multi-role Fledgling J-2s, probably MSNs 11726 to T-1/11730, on Curtiss-Wright Sales Order S.O.120. The first three came in at a total of $41,700. The six received AM trainer serials 15 to 20 (following on after the Wild WT43Ds). These were followed by three more between June 13 and 16, 1934 (at $49,575 – the reason for the significantly higher cost is not clear, probably MSNs T-2/11731 to T-4/11733). Serial number 15 was lost on March 16, 1934, and was apparently replaced by one of the second batch as MSN 15a.

Factory-posed, brand-new Curtiss Fledgling J-2, one of the first batch of three for Colombia delivered in 1931. Note the posts on either side of the rear pit for a flexible 7mm Browning (or Colt) M-2 and the blast tube for a similar gun on the top of the engine cowling.

A truly eclectic assembly of Curtiss aircraft in the main hangar at Cali. Besides Cyclone Falcon AM 113, also visible is Curtiss Fledgling J-2 AM 17, which had arrived in 1931.

The AM Fledglings received almost continuous use, including blind-flying training, as seen in this example, either MSN 18 or 19. Although armament installations were permanent, and they may have been used for gunnery training, they did not take part in operations. Note the absence of the national insignia on the power lower wing.

AM cadets celebrating graduation with a rather odd Fledging, minus its engine, in the right background. The aircraft appears to have an additional torsion strut affixed to the undercarriage and extending to the upper-forward fuselage.

Mounting 240hp Wright R-760-E Whirlwind engines, these aircraft were similar to U.S. Navy N2C-2s, except for the engines, armament, a Harrison C-2291 oil cooler for tropical conditions, and a 3.5-gallon oil tank. At Colombian insistence, the aircraft had *permanent* armament capability, consisting of a fixed, synchronized 7mm Browning M-2, an identical weapon on two special gun mounts (just visible in one of the photos), and two A-3 bomb racks capable of mounting what were described as "10 miniature bombs," probably 20-pound antipersonnel weapons.

The number 2 aircraft was test flown prior to delivery at Buffalo by Curtiss pilot H. L. Child and observed on behalf of the Colombian government by Lieutenant Commander James H. Strong, and, with one crew and all specified equipment, achieved a maximum speed of 117mph.

The Fledglings rendered sterling service to the AM and five remained on strength with the FAC by February 5, 1943, MSN 15 having been lost as noted. Of these, FAC 16 was damaged and MSN was unserviceable but repairable, while FAC 17, 19, and 20 were still in daily use. Incredibly, although three survived to pass to the Civil Aviation School at Madrid by September 11, 1946, one soldiered on with the FAC until stricken around May 1950.

But What About *Ricaurte*?

A single 435hp Curtiss D-12-powered Curtiss Falcon, MSN 10877 – unique in being mounted on a central float, with wing-tip stabilizing outriggers – was actually acquired by a popular subscription in Colombia in 1928 for $21,000.

Named *Ricaurte* for a Colombian patriot[4] of the independence movement, and although bearing Colombian national insignia, this aircraft was nominally the property of a serving AM pilot, then Teniente Benjamin Mendez R.

The young aviator planned to make a 4,600-mile "Goodwill" flight from New York to his homeland – the first such flight-delivery of an aircraft directly from the U.S. His flight to Colombia was not without incident, however. After making a planned stop for fuel at the U.S. Coco Solo Naval Air Station in the Panama Canal Zone, he hit a submerged object on take-off and his ambitions almost came to an end. He had the good fortune, however, to enjoy the hospitality and considerable expertise of the U.S. Navy who, in short order, carried out the recovery of his severely damage aircraft and arranged its repair, in cooperation with the nearby USAAC Panama Air Depot at France Field, Canal Zone.

On his take-off, after the extensive repairs – for which the U.S. charged his supporters only actual costs – he carefully watched a Navy tender clearing the waterway ahead of him, and he proceeded on to Cartagena without further incident, although some accounts claim he suffered three other mishaps along the way. Thus, chronologically, while "delivered" to Colombia in 1928, this unique aircraft could

The solitary Curtiss D-12-powered Curtiss Falcon ever mounted on a central float, although bearing Colombian national insignia in this image, the aircraft was actually owned, via a popular subscription, by AM Tte. Benjamin Mendez as of November 1928. He sold it to the AM in 1931.

Narrowly avoiding tragedy, the unique *Ricaurte*, named for a Colombian patriot, was nearly sunk in a take-off accident during the Goodwill delivery flight in November 1928 at Coco Solo Naval Air Station, Panama Canal Zone. Here, USN crews assist Mendez in salvaging the aircraft.

not as yet be counted on the AM Order of Battle and, in fact, it was not "sold" by Mendez to the AM until 1931, when it eventually gained AM MSN 111.

Camouflaged by the time of the Leticia emergency in the individualistic multicolor schemes worn by many of the combat aircraft utilized by what became known as the *Escuadrilla Aérea del Sur*, the aircraft was in fact armed. Tragically, she was lost without a trace on June 2, 1933, while en route from the Girardot, Caquetá region to the seaplane base at Flandes, while being flown by Capitán Nicolas Esguerra.

The AM toyed with additional acquisitions between 1928 and 1932, some of which bordered on the bizarre. The little-known Andiz Corporation of Ontario, California, reported that it had sold five of its rather ungainly Trojans to Colombia, and that they were to be delivered by December 1, 1929. Fitted with 115hp Kinner K5B engines and described as "two-place, cabin monoplanes," so far as can be determined, the company succumbed to the stock market crash before they could be finished.

These modest acquisitions, enjoyed by a small but competent cadre of professional officers, NCOs, and mechanics, but stymied by a politically imposed French Aviation Mission, had little idea that within two years their service would be transformed into the most powerful air arm in all of Latin America.

The camouflage applied to many of the combat aircraft was, in the case of the Hawks and Falcons, applied in completely random patterns of greens, browns, blues and red hues, directly over the aluminum dope in which they were delivered. Here, AM 111a (111 had been used on the lost D-12 powered *Ricaurte*) reveals that the sliding canopy cover for the pilot was often removed in service. Note the addition of a rather oddly shaped ventral fin, installed in-country to improve water handling.

The Potential Game Changer: Enter the Junkers Ju 52/3m

Undoubtedly dazzled by the SCADTA experience with a variety of sturdy and reliable Junkers types, and with growing German influence within the headquarters of the AM staff, it is perhaps not surprising that the AM became one of the first customers for three bomber/transport versions – Ju 52/3mdes MSN 4010 to 4012 – all delivered sometime after April 25, 1933, becoming AM 621 to 623. These were all capable of being mounted on huge twin floats, and each could mount dual 7mm guns in both a forward and an aft dorsal gun ring. These were followed by three more, Ju 52/3mg4es MSN 4031, 4032, and 4034, around May 1933, which became AM 624 to 626.

The AM had, in fact, attempted to order as many as 12 of the armed Ju 52s, with which they envisaged being able to sweep all Peruvian opposition, but German internal orders took precedence, as Hitler rearmed.

Two were lost between initial deliveries in 1932 and May 1950, when the last was finally retired, but not to combat causes. Between January 1936 and August 1941, the four survivors (FAC 621, 622, 625, and 626) amassed a remarkable record, with FAC 626 leading, having flown by that date some 1,005:15 hours, total time, in more than 627 flights, many of them into the Leticia zone and other equally remote areas under very difficult conditions.

The Americans were surprised to find significant numbers of German aircraft when they arrived. Ju 52/3m AM 622 was probably MSN 4011 and had been in the country since April 1933. It survived as FAC 622 well into 1948.

Two of the first three AM Junkers Ju 52/3mdes on their beaching gear on the ramp at Palanquero, numbers 623 (nearest) and 621. Note that their floats had both been camouflaged, although apparently, none of the aircraft themselves were so treated.

Dramatic Growth

The *Aviación Militar*, as of the fall of 1932, was thus an extremely modest organization – a social club, really. The French officer mentioned earlier, Commandant Pierre Châteauvieux (often cited in error in Colombian accounts as "Chatovieauz"), had been nominal head of the *Escuela de Aviación Militar* (EMA) at Madrid (about 18 miles northwest of Bogotá) since 1930. He had been given notice that his contract, which constituted the second French Aviation Mission to Colombia and which was to expire in December 1932, would not be renewed.

The reasons for this action were cited as a budgetary reduction, but in reality, the French officer had a truly thankless task set before him. Personal frictions and jealousy played a part, and one of Châteauvieux's friends, a Congressman named Alirio Gómez Picón, raised the specter of incompetence in the General Staff, which would not recognize the importance of the emerging science of aeronautics, and who were also accused of padding military payrolls. The Minister of War, one of the accused, General Anibal Angel, while conceding that Châteauvieux was an expert aviator, bluntly stated that he was nonetheless "not an efficient instructor," and that he had failed to instill discipline at the EMA – a charge very common throughout Latin America, where French missions were widely engaged in the 1920s and 1930s.

But Angel didn't stop there. He charged that Châteauvieux had been negligent of his contracted duties and was actually little more than an agent for a French aircraft manufacturer. Worst of all, and factually, he charged that in two years on duty, Châteauvieux had not awarded a single pilot brevet to any Colombian EMA cadet. For his part, the besieged French officer retorted that he had not been granted the aircraft or facilities he had recommended, nor the authority to act as needed, and flatly denied that he represented any French manufacturer.

There followed what was described as a "lively debate" over this issue in the House of Representatives, during which insults and rude phrases were cast about. Congressman Picón called General Gregorio Victoria an ignoramus, unprepared for his high position, while other congressmen labeled the poor Commandant Châteauvieux, who had only marginal Spanish, alternatively a "parvenu" and a "castaway," as well as an embezzler of public funds.

The upshot of all of this was that the French Mission, consisting of the one unfortunate officer and a single engineer, was sent home, and that the Colombians intended to depend upon their own pilots to rectify the situation at the EMA – a task that they almost certainly were not prepared for.

A number of outspoken AM officers recognized the emerging power of neighboring Peru and that Colombia

Known as "El Jefe" at the Cartagena base, this is believed to be none other than Capitán German Olano himself, standing before one of the Dornier Do J Wals acquired by the AM via SCADTA. He was lost in the crash of Junkers W 34h MSN 406 on July 28, 1935, at El Retiro, Huila, while en route from Palanquero to Tres Esquinas. German trained, he was one of the most highly regarded aviators in the AM.

possessed few means to counter that threat. At almost the same time, the efficiency and professionalism of the German-run SCADTA airline, equipped almost entirely with Junkers all-metal aircraft, afforded the country what amounted to a reserve-force-in-being.

The collegiality of the AM and SCADTA organizations within the tightly knit Colombian aviation community, and the SCADTA recognition that further ingratiating themselves to the ruling elite would be a politic gesture in the growing climate of tensions with Peru, proved beneficial for all concerned.

Starting in September 1932, at least four (and possibly five) float-equipped Junkers F 13s, one Dornier Wal, a single Junkers W 33 and nine assorted Junkers W 34Ls and W 34hs took on AM colors and serials, and were crewed jointly by German SCADTA and AM crews.

These were joined shortly thereafter by the first of three new Dornier Do J Wal IId flying boats, giving the AM, for the first time, the ability to project national power into the Leticia region – and perhaps beyond, a fact not lost on the Peruvian intelligence apparatus.

There has been considerable confusion regarding the number of Wals actually engaged by the AM during the conflict. The SCADTA passenger-configured Wal, "Colombia," formerly I-AZDD and civil registered in Colombia as C-28, was the first acquired, was camouflaged, and issued AM serial 601. Most sources credit the AM with acquiring only two "military" Do J Wal IIds, as AM 603 (MSN 221/34) and 604 (MSN 222/35). In fact, the AM acquired two with BMW engines (one at $86,338 and the other $89,479) as well as two more with Curtiss Conqueror engines at $97,202.56 each. These became AM 602 to 605. Of these, 602 was on strength by April 17, 1933.

And Then the Junkers K 43

Besides the converted F 13s, W 33 and W 34s noted above, most of which were acquired from SCADTA, the company also helped the AM arrange one of the most significant acquisitions of the entire conflict, via the Berlin firm of *Transaérea Técnica*. These were the three Junkers K 43dos (MSNs 2571, 2572, and 2573), which arrived on November 5, 9, and 16, 1932, respectively.

The second of the three Junkers K 43dos delivered to the AM in November 1932, serial 402, among her other accomplishments, was credited with making an urgent combat flight from Palanquero to Manaos on March 24, 1934, piloted by Tte. José I. Forero F. and Erich Rettich. This was, eventually, the most heavily utilized aircraft of the trio.

Probably AM 401, this K 43do wears the dazzling camouflage applied to most aircraft operating in the Leticia zone, and the underwing bomb racks can just be discerned. Oddly, this aircraft does not appear to have the national insignia applied.

The U.S. Embassy had learned, on February 27, 1933, that the situation was potentially worse than just the initial trio of K 43s. Joaquin Samper, an import broker, had informed H. P. Macgowan, the Acting Commercial Attaché, that the AM had in fact decided to standardize on the K 43 series as their preferred bombardment type, and further, that the Ju 52/3m series was to be designated as the standardized transport type.

The good news was that Samper also informed them that the AM had also decided, at the same time, to standardize on the Curtiss Sea Hawk for pursuit duties and either the Curtiss Falcon or Helldiver for all observation, attack, and light bombardment assignments, and that an array of Curtiss types was to equip the training establishment. In the process, the AM specifically rejected the two Martin T4M-1s offered via the Detroit Aircraft Corporation which, on reflection, was actually the best decision.

SCADTA, which represented Junkers, reinforced the Minister of War's decision to go with the array of K 43s and Ju 52/3ms, with the astonishing claim that Pan American Airways was going to buy and use Ju 52/3ms itself, and the AM choice of the type was thus in consonance with the world's foremost long-distance airline!

Sr. Samper, while knowing full well that this assertion was simply not true, did not see fit to deny it in the face of the Minister of War, but did rush to the U.S. Embassy to verify that it was, in fact, a false claim. Apparently, the Embassy was able to verify that the claim was false, as the initial AM orders for K 43s stopped at just the three aircraft.

Issued AM serials 401 to 403, these rugged warplanes were, ironically, equipped with American engines, 600hp Pratt & Whitney R-1340-S3H1 Wasps and fairly bristled with guns: twin 7.9mm

With camouflage removed (or never applied?), K 43do AM 403 is seen here being operated as a pure transport, without the speed ring on the engine, with the dorsal gun position fairing in place, but with camouflaged floats.

Madsen guns, in a dorsal position (and a third, ventral hatch position for a single gun, which was seldom used)[5] and racks for bombs under both the fuselage center-line and the wings. Some reports state that the pilot also had a fixed 7.9mm gun for his use as well, but this has escaped verification. The K 43's guns posed a slight logistics problem, as the majority of the U.S. aircraft acquired used 7mm Browning M-2s, and armorers were constantly enjoined to ensure that the right ammunition was distributed to the right guns. As insurance, the AM purchased some 8,600 rounds of 7.9mm ammunition with the aircraft. Oddly, the three aircraft were apparently different in detail, as the first two cost $40,955.47, while the third came in at $41,565.73. All had twin floats and had underwing racks for up to eight 110-pound bombs. However, the AM is known to have ordered the following weapons from *Transaérea Técnica* in Berlin at precisely the same time as the K 43s, and they may well have been intended for possible use on these aircraft:

        50 = 100kg high-explosive bombs
        125 = 50kg "mine bombs"
        500 = 25kg high-explosive bombs
        1,250 = 12kg high-explosive bombs
        1,000 = 3kg high-explosive bombs

All three K 43s survived as late as March 1942, and of these, FAC 402 was by far the most heavily utilized, while, by August 1941, FAC 403 had apparently experienced some problems, as she had amassed a total of only 13:50 hours in five flights since January 1936.

Chapter 3
The Curtiss-Wright Connection

While the seconded SCADTA aircraft and the new Wals had augmented the nation's air arm at a fortuitous juncture, the AM, spurred on unquestionably by able Curtiss-Wright overtures and the ever-present potential for generous commissions as war clouds gathered, had essentially been sold on the need for a truly well-rounded air force. Seldom recognized, the principal personality representing Curtiss-Wright in Colombia through all that followed was the very-well-connected Sr. Joaquín Samper H.[1] via his agency, Urueta y Samper H. (Sucs.). Samper exercised integrity during this transaction by seeking the approval of Curtiss-Wright, with whom he had an exclusive contract. Perhaps to his surprise, Curtiss-Wright did not object to the sale. Curtiss-Wright was determined to almost singlehandedly provide that force.

Besides the Curtiss aircraft described earlier, and which had rendered excellent service to the conventional AM force, between October 1932 and June 1934, the AM acquired no fewer than 61 Curtiss-Wright aircraft,[2] starting with five Curtiss Model 35-A Sea Hawk Type I float-equipped, single-seat fighter-bombers in October and November 1932.

The Model 35-As (MSNs SH1/11653 to SH6/11658) were the F-16s of their day. Issued AM serials 801 to 804 (one was lost to a crash before gaining a serial), they were fitted with Wright R-1820-F Cyclone engines, and after being erected and tested by the newly arrived American airmen who were at the center of this account, they immediately became the pride of the service. Especially noteworthy, compared to the sturdy but lumbering Junkers types, was the pretty incredible take-off and flight

One of the original Curtiss Model 35-A Sea Hawk Type Is for Colombia before the modifications to the rudder and ventral fin were added as a result of actual service in the field. Note that the A-3 bomb racks were installed already but no cowling has been fitted.

Model 35-A Sea Hawk Type I serial 803 was one of the first delivered, and had been camouflaged and mounted on floats – and was almost certainly one of those dispatched south. Here, circa 1934, she has been doped aluminum overall once again, returned to wheels, and is being flown out of the bush by U.S. pilot Jesse Rothrock, minus wheel spats and fairings, after a cadet had made a forced landing.

performance for the day. With a full load of fuel, guns, ammunition, and light bombs on the underwing A-3 racks, the aircraft got off the water in eight seconds and then, at 1,950rpm and 900 feet – seldom exceeded in the combat zone – turned in a top speed, corrected, of 189.56mph.

True to form, the Curtiss sales team suggested the versatile, multi-role Curtiss-Wright C14R Osprey as a perfect complement to the new Hawks. Three of these arrived in December 1932 and were issued AM serials 121 to 123. Unfortunately, the MSNs have not been traced. Although a follow-up order for as many as ten more was expected, and two sets of twin-pontoons were actually acquired for those on hand, the loss of two of the Ospreys in accidents within a short time following delivery, and the relatively modest armament package they could bring to bear compared to the far more militant Falcons that Curtiss was offering at virtually the same time, convinced the AM to divert their funds to these aircraft instead of more C14Rs. One of the Ospreys soldiered on into July 1939, however.

The Ospreys, in truth, which committed themselves very well indeed in Bolivia during the Chaco War (1932–35) and elsewhere, had fallen victim to the very central problem that heralded the eventual arrival of the American Mission, the pivotal event, as it turned out, of this entire epoch.

On Wednesday afternoon, February 8, 1933, a young AM officer named Tte. Guillermo Zornosa (also given as Zarnosa) had crashed one of the aircraft, barely two months old, at Girardot, and died in the flames after the aircraft hit the ground. He had been a visiting cadet at the Argentine *Escuela de Aviación Militar* (EMA) at El Palomar but had been recalled home due to the emergency, having arrived only a week before the crash.

The Osprey he was flying – for the first time – was apparently float-equipped, as he had taken off from the river (this was apparently his very first flight in a float-equipped aircraft). According to witnesses, however, before he had gained sufficient altitude or flying speed, he attempted a sharp turn, stalled, and went straight into the ground. The newspapers made much of the accident and laid blame on the aircraft, but it was obviously very much a case of unfamiliarity with the type and inexperience. But the C14R series was blacklisted by the AM as a direct result, a type which otherwise would have almost certainly proven of great utility.

This loss was followed, in short order, by word that Mayor Mendez himself had crashed in a Curtiss Sea Hawk near the Caucayá River in the combat zone on Saturday afternoon, February 4. The Colombian newspapers once more attacked the Curtiss products, claiming to have learned, somehow, that the cables to the rudder had not functioned properly, and that the fuel lines had become clogged – the latter a distinct possibility, given the primitive circumstances under which the aircraft were being fueled and serviced.

Mendez was rushed by plane back to Bogotá in a Junkers F 13 flown by none other than Mayor Herbert Boy himself to be hospitalized, and was in fact visited by Sylvester Roll, the Assistant Trade Commissioner assigned to the U.S. Embassy. He found that the pilot had suffered a broken leg, concussions, and other minor injuries. When asked by Roll what had actually happened, he reportedly said that

I haven't the least idea what happened – as a matter of fact, I barely remember getting into the plane! I do not remember the take-off, nor do I have the least idea what happened thereafter. The Hawk is an excellent plane, as a matter of fact, it is too good! The pontoon equipment makes the plane very difficult to handle, and unless one is wide awake every minute, there is danger of going into a tail spin. I don't, in any sense of the word, blame the Hawk for my accident.

Mendez had in fact crashed into the jungle, not far from the river, but even at that, and a testament to the terrain surrounding the zone of operations, it took searchers 4 ½ hours, including searches by air, to find the crash site. Rescuers found him still in the cockpit, unconscious, and the engine was half-buried in the muck. In retrospect, Mendez held that crashing into the jungle had saved his life and that, had it not been for the yellow in the national insignia on his very effectively camouflaged Sea Hawk, they may have never found him.

Not long after the Ospreys and initial batch of Sea Hawks entered into the AM inventory, a most unusual addition to the force arrived. Just after Christmas, on December 28, 1932, a brand-new Consolidated P2Y-1C Commodore flying

Rothrock and Nobile next to two of the 29 Hawks which staged through Cali. These two officers specialized in pursuit aviation training. Note the auxiliary slip fuel tank under the fuselage.

boat patrol bomber – which must certainly have attracted the notice of Peruvian agents – landed. It was followed, by mid-January 1933, by a second, and then a third arrived later, apparently around April 27. The first two were hastily camouflaged and issued AM serials 611, 612, and 614 (613 seems to have been skipped, perhaps for superstitious reasons!).

Colombia acquired the first of two very competent Consolidated P2Y-1C Commodore flying boats in December 1932 as part of her enormous expansion program. Formerly X-2102 (MSN 1), serial 611 remained in service as late as 1948! The roundel under the starboard wing appears to be non-standard.

Still doped aluminum overall, and wearing U.S. Experimental License X-2102 – but with Colombian national insignia – the first of three Consolidated P2Y-1Cs for the AM had just completed acceptance tests at Buffalo when pictured. She was camouflaged almost immediately upon arrival in Colombia.

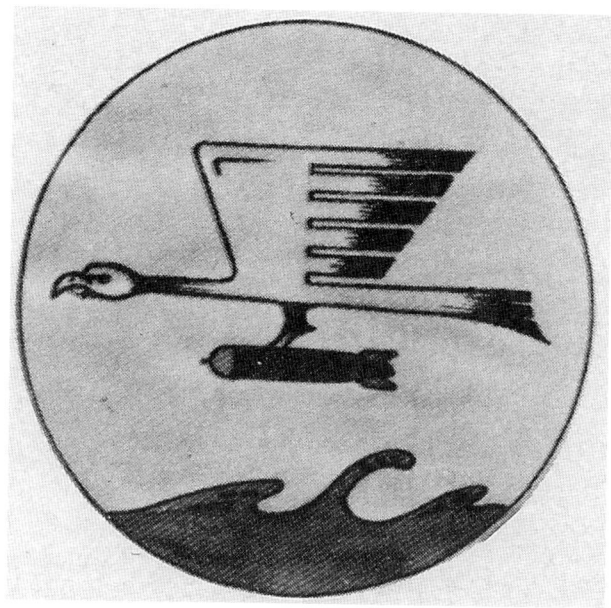

This insignia is known to have been painted onto at least one of the three Consolidated P2Y-1C Commodore flying boats acquired by the AM and is self-explanatory. The P2Y-1Cs may have been acquired to counter the formidable Peruvian Navy, which the Colombians fully expected to encounter in some manner if hostilities developed.

Consolidated only admitted to selling one P2Y-1C to Colombia,[3] MSN 1, and the identities of the other two have escaped verification. These large, capable aircraft, viewed by the Colombians as strategic bombers during the crisis period, rendered excellent service. Two must have been lost at some point, and remain unreported, but one soldiered on as late as September 1946.

The P2Y-1Cs have repeatedly been cited as having been "Colombian Navy" aircraft. However, the Navy did not acquire its own aircraft until after WWII, and this assumption has probably been fueled by the insignia applied by crews to at least one of the aircraft, which retrospectively has been labeled as being that of the *Grupo de Apoyo Tactico Aero-Naval*. Interestingly, the P2Y-1Cs were piloted almost exclusively by Germans, including Friedrich-Karl Maringer, with Colombian gunners.

German Agitation Against American Equipment

By February 16, 1933, despite the fact that German crews were flying several of the Model 35-A Sea Hawks under combat conditions in the south (and where one, AM 801, was lost to one of their number), certain SCADTA officials were openly bucking American aircraft as often as possible to any audience that mattered.

Indeed, the newly arrived P2Y-1C, which the AM very much wanted to make operational and send to the combat zone, was still in component parts in their hangar at Barranquilla, where the crews who had been contracted to assemble it were going about the task in a very leisurely fashion, at best. Herr Kuehl, the SCADTA manager in Bogotá, was conducting nearly all of the company negotiations with the AM, and told officers of the U.S. Embassy that "now you have got your Consolidated plane here – and what are you going to do with it without a crew to take charge of it?" Ernesto Samper had actually been the agent for Consolidated on the acquisition, and was frustrated by the total lack of cooperation on erecting the aircraft. He had found the wire cables for the bomb racks completely unserviceable because of exposure at Barranquilla to salt water and salt air corrosion for more than a month – but he also contended that their deteriorating condition could have been due to acid having been poured onto them.

Shining light on the matter apparently had the desired effect, however, as by February 18, the P2Y-1C was finished and, although being piloted by a mixed German (Hans Dietrich Hoffmann in particular) and AM (Posada) crew familiar with large flying boats, included two Americans as well – a man named Lee as the radio operator and another named Killilea as crew chief.

This was very serious business, at a very crucial moment. So much so, in fact, that Joaquin Samper, the Curtiss front man, demanded an investigation of SCADTA's activities. This sort of thing was the last thing the AM needed at this point.

Having been prepared for the combat zone, this is Curtiss Model 35-A Sea Hawk Type I AM 805, MSN SH6/11658, which arrived around January 9, 1933, and may have seen action in the *Zona del Sur*.

Curtiss Model 65 Sea Hawk Type II AM 813 (MSN SH17/11756), delivered around June 30, 1933, has clearly experienced trauma, the cause of which is unknown. Note that the Townend ring is also missing.

Chapter 4
Colombia Attacks

By February 17, 1933, while the EMA was attempting to chart its own course and, hopefully actually graduate some trained airmen, the situation in Leticia had escalated. The first clash between regular Peruvian and Colombian forces had taken place at Tarapacá, between February 14 and 17, 1933, just west of the Brazilian boundary on the Putumayo and 140km north of Leticia. The Colombian force, consisting of the river gunboats *Córdoba*, *Mosquera*, *Pechincha*, *Bogotá*, and flagship *Barranquilla*, supported by two transports (*Boyacá* and *Narino*), with something near 1,000 troops, entered the Putumayo heading north from the Amazon, exercised a warning via radio, and notified the Peruvian garrison that they were intent on retaking the area.

The commander of the Colombian expedition dispatched a young second lieutenant around 0800 on February 14, under a flag of truce, to actually deliver the ultimatum demanding surrender, to which the ranking Peruvian officer replied that he had to consult with his superiors – which would require several days, as they were a considerable distance away and could not be reached quicker.

Probably unaware of all of this on the ground, at 0955, the Peruvians replied to the Colombian force by dispatching four aircraft (some sources state only two, Vought O2U-1E Corsairs), led by Cdr. Montoya, while still in Brazilian territory and, according to most reports, one of the vessels, apparently the gunboat *Córdoba*, experienced a near-miss by a bomb. Shortly thereafter, a Colombian air detachment of three Curtiss Model 35-A Sea Hawk Type Is arrived from an advance base at La Pedrera[1] under none other than Mayor Herbert Boy and obliged the Peruvian aircraft to vacate the area. So far as can be determined, this was the first aerial engagement of the unfolding conflict between opposing aircraft, and no claims were made by either side, although one account claims that Herbert Boy himself managed somehow to get airborne in the short interval between spotting the O2U-1Es and their attack on the fleet and caused them to jettison their bombs over the jungle. The same account claims that the guns on his aircraft jammed, due to the fact that the ammunition was Colombian-made, which seems highly improbable. One account, however, stated that Tte. Francisco Secada, after dropping his bombs from an O2U-1E coded 5-E-6, and thus being freed from the extra weight, engaged the nimble Sea Hawks head-on and thus covered the retreat of his comrades.

The following day, February 15, at around 0730, the Colombian "fleet" proceeded upriver under aerial cover, alleged to have included a loitering, camouflaged Dornier Wal flying boat, where they

Rarely illustrated, a CAP Curtiss Cyclone Falcon (XXXII-83-3) and one of at least two Vought O2U-3B Corsairs (XXXII-83-2). Note that both aircraft have bomb racks under their wings and that the O2U-3B has two fixed guns in the upper wing. Her engine cowl is painted in sections of red and white, suggesting this was a flight leader's aircraft.

commenced bombarding Tarapacá and, at about 0800, were joined in the attack by Colombian aircraft. The Peruvians returned fire, apparently with one 75mm Krupp gun (and six others described as including "mountain artillery," plus, a number of machine guns), but evacuated aboard the river launch *La Estefita* during the night of the 14th upriver to Cotuhé and, leaving their heavy guns to be captured by the Colombians on the morning of the 15th, the abandoned citizens of the town surrendered. Amazingly, there had not been a single fatality on either side, although some Peruvians were wounded.

General Alfredo Vásquez Cobo, leading the victorious Colombians, then set out to attack Leticia itself, and was reinforced with six additional aircraft.[2] These were reportedly based at a place called Fonte Boa, some 550km east of Leticia. The Peruvians, for their part, had flown as many aircraft as could be scrapped together to Iquitos and Caballococha – some reports stating as many as 40, although this is hardly credible. The Peruvians were also reportedly preparing an elaborate fortification and trench system around Leticia, which must have been a truly thankless job under the prevailing circumstances, to defend against the expected attack.

As the clerk in charge of the Military Attaché's office in the U.S. Embassy in Bogotá, A. E. Milmore sanguinely reported, "so far it looks like a comic-opera war." Peru and Colombia, rather belatedly, severed diplomatic relations on February 14.

On February 18, 1933, CAP Stearman C-3R 4-E-3, one of ten acquired in 1930, being flown by Tte. Elias Moreno, and escorted by Tte. Gal'lindo in an O2U-1E, departed Iquitos on a mission to fly a load of medicines and a radio to the Peruvian garrison at Güepi, one of the few C-3Rs ever mounted on floats. After the intrepid flight of this unarmed aircraft into a very active combat zone had completed its mission, the two aircraft started their take-off run from the Putumayo – and came under intense ground fire from the nearby Colombian forces. The C-3R managed to escape with some slight damage, but the O2U-1E was hit and burst into flames, crashing into the river. The crew escaped, however.

Through all of this, the Colombian AM unit in the zone, which, as noted earlier, had been designated as the *Escuadrilla Aérea del Sur*, had consisted of a mix of the best available Colombians and a number of German pilots and crew members who had been hired away or "loaned" from SCADTA for the

One of the best buys made by the CAP was for ten hearty Stearman C-3Rs delivered after April 1930. Fitted with R-760 Whirlwind engines, at least one of these, 4-E-3, visible in this line-up, came under fire while operating on floats near Güepi, but escaped.

emergency. These included four Germans – Capitáns Hans Wermer von Engel, von Oertzen, F. Tesseas von Heydebreck, and Fritz von Donop – and at least four AM officers – Capitán Andrés M. Díaz, Teniente José Ignacio Forero, and Subtenientes Luis A. Garcia Bonilla and César Abadia – these latter constituting the majority of the best fliers in the entire AM at the time. These crews piloted at least four of the brand-new Model 35-A Hawk Type Is and a mix of hastily armed Junkers F 13s, the W 33 and W 34hs. The German contributions to this series of actions was widely heralded throughout Colombia, and certainly did not tarnish the reputation of SCADTA in the process.

Meanwhile, back at Buenaventura, commencing in January 1933 and trailing off into the end of March, six more Curtiss Model 35-A Hawk Type Is arrived, were assembled, tested, and partially fitted with floats or wheel undercarriages. These were SH6/11658 and SH10/11701 to SH14/11705, and they gained AM serials 805 to 810 on S.O. 117.

Back in the combat zone, two further actions took place, one of them on March 17 at 1430 near a small settlement of Ticuna natives, about a three-hour march from a place called Buenos Aires on the Rio Cotuhé, which is almost in the center of the 4,000 square miles that formed the Leticia trapezoid and about 30 air miles southwest of Tarapacá. The Colombians had gone up the river with the gunboat *Córdoba* and apparently attacked a detachment of about 50 Peruvians, who hastily abandoned their positions. Peruvian casualties are unknown, but the Colombians lost one man killed and five wounded. At 1700, six Peruvian aircraft attacked the *Córdoba* but apparently without effect, but one Peruvian aircraft was seen to be trailing smoke and falling from return fire.

It had become clear very quickly to the AM that its combat detachments in the Leticia area required nearly constant and expedient resupply of parts, ammunition, fuel, and the necessities of life, and so measures were set in motion to augment the service's rather meager air transport capabilities by essentially commandeering nearly all of the capable transport aircraft remaining in the country. This included a solitary Hamilton H-45 Metalplane, operated on floats by the Andian Nacional Corporation, but which had been locally brought up to H-47 standard by the installation of a 420hp engine. This aircraft, MSN 58 (and formerly NC-466E) – named *Aguila II* and issued

Among other duties when they first arrived, the U.S. Group was tasked with test-flying the Curtiss aircraft as they were assembled. National insignia and serials had yet to be painted on.

MSN 205 – was handed over to military crews around February 17, 1933. As it was not reported after May 1933, it is assumed to have been lost in some unknown incident in the south.

There is some evidence that this aircraft may have been used as an *ad hoc* ambulance aircraft to and from the south as, by April 15, 1933, the Red Cross had somehow been enlisted to start a drive to acquire "additional" ambulance planes for use during the conflict. Apparently SCADTA, learning of this, offered to make two of the new Junkers Ju 52/3ms available to the Red Cross for ambulance work, rather than see yet more new American aircraft introduced into the equation.

At almost precisely the same time, the Colombian Consul in New York received an unsolicited overture on February 14, 1933, from, of all places, the Detroit Aircraft Export Corporation, advising that they could make available two 1928-vintage Martin T4M-1 torpedo bombers, complete with floats, for delivery in three weeks for $59,500, including "special equipment," although the nature of that special equipment was not defined. The Colombian Consul, acting on his government's expressed desire to acquire as many capable aircraft as quickly as possible, recommended the purchase of these two aircraft, which must be assumed to have been surplus from the U.S. Navy. The Ministry of War in Bogotá disapproved the purchase on February 27, however, on the grounds that the two aircraft had been found to have been used in tests and had more than 60 hours' flying time, and may thus have been stressed at some point.

By February 24, 1933, the Brazilians, who quite rightly had grown concerned about all of these hostilities taking place on the waters of the Amazon (for which all parties held navigation rights), but

As Peruvian and Colombian elements approached combat far up the Amazon, and in proximity to Brazilian territory, the Brazilian Navy dispatched major surface units to defend its territory and neutrality, including the "airplane carrier" *AdoB Distrito Federal*, which carried two dismantled Fairey Gordon Mk.IIIs, which could be assembled, with some effort, and winched overboard to operate on floats.

deep in the heart of their own national territory, were struggling to determine whether either party had violated Brazilian territory. General Almério da Moura, Brazilian Army commander of the 8th Corps Area, who had his flag temporarily at Manaos, told the press that he had sufficient Brazilian forces at his disposal to ensure Brazilian neutrality, if necessary.

The Peruvians, whether intentionally or by accident, very nearly were first to violate this neutrality. Following an attempt to escape downriver in a launch (which they had dignified by calling it a "gunboat") below Tabatinga, without making the customary notification to the Brazilian authorities, General da Moura ordered the two side-passages or navigable canals of the upper Amazon at that point to be closed, restricting the vessel to the main channel of the river, which was neutral.

The Brazilians had become so concerned that they had dispatched the First Division of the Brazilian Navy from Rio as early as January, and this powerful unit (which included the "airplane carrier" *AdoB Distrito Federal*, which might more accurately be described as an "aircraft tender") was holding station at Pará, awaiting developments upriver. They did dispatch a number of Brazilian naval aircraft north in mid-February, but this did not end well, as a number of them came to grief en route and two, which had passed through Bahia, were stranded at a point on coast of Maranhão. Repair crews had been sent to locate and repair the aircraft, and then they were to have continued on their way to surveil the Peruvian and Colombian activities. In addition to these aircraft, which have remained unidentified, three Navy Vought V-66B Corsairs (designated O2Vs in Brazilian Navy service), had been fitted with floats, tested for more than 20 hours, and dispatched to reinforce the Brazilian contingent on the upper Amazon.

While all of these behind-the-scenes transactions were occurring, the conflict continued to unfold in the south of Colombia. The next action of note came on March 25, 1933, at dawn on the Peruvian garrison at Güepi (consisting of five humble dwellings) in Peruvian territory about 40 miles above Caucayá, on the right bank of the upper Putumayo and, thus, about 425 air miles northwest of Tarapacá, an exceedingly remote location for action of any sort. The gunboats *Cartagena* and *Santa Marta* bombarded the hapless village for not less than eight hours, aided by six AM[3] aircraft, which somehow managed to locate the action. The surviving Peruvians then fled the scene, leaving behind ten dead and several wounded. The Colombian casualties amounted to four soldiers dead and seven wounded. The Colombians also took 24 prisoners, among them one *Teniente*, as well as some machine guns, rifles, and ammunition. The Peruvian garrison had been estimated at 500 officers and men, but this may have been a Colombian exaggeration.

The Reluctant Field Marshal?

In the midst of all of this, General Anibal Angel, the Colombian Chief of Staff, accompanied by Coronel de Artillería Josué Tavera and Comandante Tobias Lopez Mejica, departed Bogotá on April 15 for Europe – a rather inopportune moment to be absent from the country, on reflection – to buy more arms in a shopping spree which was to cover several countries. During Angel's absence, Teniente Coronel Climaco Jaramillo became the Acting Minister of War but was, in reality, Acting Chief of Staff.

Meanwhile, in the zone of operations, General Alfredo Vasquez Cobo, the Colombian commander in the field (who, remarkably, also somehow filled the post of Colombian Minister to France at the same time), had been sojourning for more than six weeks in La Esperanza, a little railroad station at an altitude of 4,200 feet – which had, for the tropics, a rather pleasant climate – between Bogotá and Girardo, frequently coming up from the Putumayo by AM aircraft – but never once to Bogotá. His stay in La Esperanza was, at the time, surrounded by speculation and mystery. The newspapers announced on at least a dozen occasions that he was going to return to the Putumayo "the following day" to resume direct command of his deployed forces, but he never did, and no official statement as to why was ever forthcoming.

The Colombian President and the Ministers of War and the Interior paid Cobo several visits at La Esperanza, traveling there by special train, but they, too, never revealed to newsmen the gist of their conversations with the general or the substance of their lengthy conferences.

Finally, during the week of April 20, General Vasquez finally left La Esperanza for the Pacific coast, ostensibly to inspect – for reasons that challenge understanding – coastal defenses at Tumaco and Buenaventura, and then abruptly boarded the steamer S.S. *Cali* for Colon in the Panama Canal Zone, where he arrived on April 23. It was suggested that from there he would travel on to return to France on the S.S. *Colombie*, bound on an "important mission for the Colombian government." All of these movements were handled, by Colombian standards, with the greatest of secrecy, but U.S. diplomatic observers commented that they felt that the rather elderly officer had enough of the Amazon and the Putumayo jungles and was quite content to let someone else secure the glory of reconquering them for Colombia!

Meanwhile, in the Combat Zone…

Two more clashes followed the earlier incidents in quick succession – both on Easter Sunday, April 16 – but this time, the Peruvians were on the attack. One of these was some distance from Güepi,[4] the small village on the upper Putumayo which had been captured by the Colombians three weeks previously, in the direction of the Peruvian post of San Pedro Pantoja on the Napo River, about 55 air miles south of Güepi. The other was at a place called Calderón, also on the Putumayo, about 40 miles upriver from the Peruvian fort at Puerto Arturo.

The Peruvians claimed "important" victories, claiming that the Colombians near Güepi had been obliged to withdraw about 6km, and that they suffered "heavy losses in men and armaments" in the process. News published in Bogotá at first declared these statements as outright lies, but later admitted there may have been some clashes between advanced detachments, but that the Colombian troops were "holding all principal positions near Güepi." As regards the Peruvian attack on Calderón, Peru claimed that the Colombian forces lost 30 dead and substantial quantities of arms, while the official Colombian report stated that the attack was repulsed and that Colombian Army casualties consisted of but one dead and three lightly wounded, without stating whether these were officers, NCOs, or troops.

On April 24, the local newspapers in Bogotá published a telegram that they had received from the Minister of War, who was at the time in Caucayá, and dated the 22nd, which reported with some accuracy on the attack made by four CAP aircraft two or three days previously (apparently on the 19th) – it was rather vague – on the Brazilian launch *Emmita*, near the mouth of the Yaricaya River, which fed into the Putumayo, about 60 miles below Caucayá. This incident may well have drawn Brazilian forces into the conflict, as casualties aboard the launch included the first officer, killed, and the captain[5] and two of the crew were wounded. The launch then limped back to Caucayá. Built to take as much as 40 tons of freight and 30 passengers, the vessel was owned by Juan Miguel Pinto Riveiro, on whose behalf the Colombian government cabled to Rio reporting the attack. The shallow-draft vessel had been on a routine trip, carrying freight between Puerto Asis and Caucayá, and had been en route back to Brazilian destinations at the time of the attack.

By May 19, although several minor skirmishes had taken place of little importance – mainly exchanges of gunfire – the strategic situation remained unchanged. Puerto Arturo, the main Peruvian operating base, about halfway between the foothills of the Andes and the Tarapacá on the Brazilian border, had not been attacked and remained the primary obstacle preventing the Colombian gunboats *Santa Marta* and *Cartagena*, then on the upper Putumayo, from joining the rest of the Colombian river naval units on the lower Putumayo. These included the transport *Boyaca* (the former S.S. *Bridgetown*) and the seven smaller gunboats *Barranquilla*, *Cordoba* (a gunboat and former WWI German minesweeper), *Mosquera* (the former *Royal Highlander*, fitted rather crudely with two 88mm cannon), *Pichincha*, *Mariscal Sucre*, *Bogotá*, and *Colombia*, most of which had been jury-rigged with 75mm Bofors guns.

But the Colombians – as well as the Peruvians – were obviously still reinforcing their units in the zone, and improving their defenses, not to mention acquiring additional aircraft and arms wherever they could locate them. A protracted conflict and possible failure of negotiations was clearly anticipated.

On May 18, the Peruvian medium-sized transport *Marañon* was observed passing a place called Benjamin Constant on the Brazilian–Peruvian border en route to Iquitos, reportedly with no fewer than 12,000 cases of aviation fuel, ammunition, and associated aviation materiel aboard. The next day, the Peruvian Navy cruiser *Almirante Grau* arrived at Belem do Pará, accompanied by her escorts, the submarines *R-1* and *R-4*. The commander of the squadron informed Brazilian port authorities that they planned to stay three days to refuel and replenish before proceeding up the Amazon.

Other minor actions followed, but by May 23, 1933, Peru and Colombia had agreed to submit the controversy to an international commission.

Unfortunately, three days before Peru's final acceptance of the terms, the Colombian AM lost two pilots (one Colombian and one German) and three mechanics (two Colombians and one German). These men had been aboard the former SCADTA float-equipped Junkers F 13, by then serialed as 202, and was described by the Colombians following the loss as a "fighting unit," although exactly how it may have been armed is unknown.[6] The exact nature and circumstances of the loss have been in dispute ever since, and only one of the five crewmen was recovered, although part of the fuselage was. The aircraft was probably overloaded and almost certainly had been deploying bombs by tossing them out the door aperture.

At this point, despite their contributions to the Colombian cause, by June 2, 1933, and undoubtedly fueled by the unexplained loss of F 13 202, rumors were circulating publicly in Bogotá that the Germans had all but taken over the Colombian air arm. It was alleged that German pilots, both those "loaned" to the government by SCADTA as well as a number of mercenaries, had been used by (then) Coronel Herbert Boy, himself a German citizen, although resident in Colombia, and the *de facto* commander of the AM, to the total exclusion or subordination of qualified Colombian aircrews, and further, that intentional efforts had been made to discourage training for Colombians so that they might assume leadership roles. None other than a Mr. Killilea, a U.S. citizen from Buffalo, New York, who had been sent along with the solitary Consolidated P2Y-1C flying boat that the AM had acquired in December 1932 to maintain the aircraft, had been ordered by Capitán Hans Dietrich Hoffmann, a former SCADTA pilot who was the only pilot qualified on the P2Y-1C, and who, in spite of his name, was actually a Colombian citizen, not to instruct any "native" Colombians in the maintenance of the aircraft. He also stated that the crews of the various AM aircraft which had been sent to the zone of action in frantic search for the Peruvian cruiser *Grau* had been composed entirely of German pilots,[7] with the exception of two Americans, who have eluded positive identification, but one of which was almost certainly Nobile – about whom more later. He claimed that several of the German crewmen were untrained and "incompetent" and that one of the so-called German mechanics had been a car salesman in Berlin, while one of the gunner/observers, who doubled as a bombardier, had been a traveling salesman before being hired by the Colombians and that neither claimed to have had any prior aviation experience. Given the efficiency of the SCADTA crews, this seems hardly credible, and some personal grievance on the part of citizen Killilea cannot be ruled out.

The willingness of Colombia to settle the issue was undoubtedly motivated, to some extent, by the fact that, after an epic journey all the way up and around the Pacific coast of South America, through the Panama Canal, and then down the northeast "hump" of Brazil to the post of Pará, the Peruvian cruiser *Almirante Grau*, escorted by two submarines (the *R-1* and *R-4*), had arrived and made it known publicly that they were about to sail up the Amazon to the Peru–Colombia–Brazil border area and make short work of the Colombian surface units operating there. The Peruvian naval officer commanding this force had, by May 23, received no change to his orders, and was not aware of any discussions to end the conflict, and as far as he was concerned, he was still heading upriver.

The *Almirante Grau*, the first of two Peruvian cruisers so named, was a game-changer. Built in 1906 and displacing 3,200 tons and with a crew of 258, she could achieve 24 knots and had a range of 4,500 miles, and was one of the very few Latin American warships of the time to be routinely fitted with a catapult, on which she carried a CAP Vought O2U-3B Corsair. She was armed with two 155mm main guns, eight 76mm guns, eight more of 42mm, and two torpedo tubes. She had also been hastily retrofitted before her sorties to Brazil with heavy-caliber anti-aircraft machine guns. Her escorts were two rather elderly U.S. built submarines, laid down in 1926 (*R-1*) and 1928 (*R-4*), powered by twin, 500hp diesels, each with four torpedo tubes in both the bow and stern, one with a crew of 26 and other 28. The *R-1* boasted a 76mm deck gun in addition to her torpedo tubes and had a range of 8,000 miles. The *R-4* was identically outfitted, but was much slower, 9.5 knots compared to 14.5 knots for the *R-1*. One can only imagine the conditions aboard these vessels operating in the heat of the Amazon, even when surfaced. Exactly how they intended to maneuver and fight when reaching the combat zone, where their heavy armament was expected to totally overwhelm the Colombian armada, remains a mystery.

In his defense, Herbert Boy, although of German descent, describing himself as a "naturalized" and loyal Colombian, had done what needed to be done to answer the call of his nation, and the German personnel he recruited were, in fact, the best available to him at the time. At the root of all of this, however, was undoubtedly the fact that SCADTA very much wanted to retain dominance in Colombian aviation matters, and training competent Colombian pilots and crews was not very high on their agenda. Thus, for SCADTA, the Leticia conflict was little more than an opportunity for some adventure, aggrandizement and yes, profit – motives which resounded during the bleak Depression period.

Chapter 5
Curtiss-Wright Arrives in Force, Just as the Dust Settles

It was clear that the visit of Colombian Dr. Alfonso Lopez to Lima the week of May 20, 1933, led to the start of a negotiated settlement to the conflict. Indeed, both sides agreed to submit their controversy to an international commission as had been proposed by the Council of the League of Nations on March 18. A final agreement was signed on May 25 in Geneva, and Colombia sent orders to her forces in the zone to cease hostilities the same day.

What is not generally reported is that Colombia agreed to defray all of the salaries and expenses of the international commission that had been handed the thankless job of taking charge of the Leticia region. But this did not in the slightest diminish the feverish efforts that were already in motion to radically expand either Colombian or Peruvian armed forces.

SCADTA and its endorsement of German aeronautical products had unquestionably influenced – and directly benefited – the rapid evolution of the AM during most of the emergency period of the Leticia conflict, with only a relative few U.S. aircraft involved to this point. The Colombian discomfort with what they perceived as the insidious nature of Germanic influence had, however, opened the doors, as early as the fall of 1932, to the overtures of the Curtiss-Wright Export Corporation, which was never slow to recognize an opportunity. For all intents and purposes, Curtiss-Wright proceeded to transform the AM into what amounted to two separate air arms: one equipped and manned almost exclusively with very capable, state-of-the-art German-built aircraft and crews, and the other equipped overwhelmingly with Curtiss types.

Between October 31, 1932, and March 2, 1935, the AM ordered, on seven consecutive contracts, no fewer than 29 variants of the classic Hawk fighter/fighter bomber and assorted support types. These included 11 Model 35-A Sea Hawk Type Is (already described), 18 Model 65 Sea Hawk Type IIs, and one exotic Model 65-A Hawk Type II-A.

The early Model 35-As had proven to be both dependable and versatile, but the Curtiss sales force did not hesitate to note to the Colombians that they had also sold the exact same type to Peru,[1] and that their Model 65 Sea Hawk Type II, with 712hp engines, would provide the AM with an edge. The model 65 differed from the model 35-A only slightly in most instances (the floats and engine were moved forward about 4 and 3 inches, respectively, and a longer chord speed ring was installed to accommodate the larger engine, very similar to that on U.S. Navy F11C-2s). But the key recognition device was the necessary addition of a ventral fin at the bottom of the fuselage on float-equipped examples to improve handling on the water and the provision of two fuselage fuel tanks increasing fuel capacity – and thus range – to 94 gallons. While the Model 35-A used the R-1820-F engine, the Model 65s mounted the improved SR-1820F-2. They both used Edo Type 4546 floats with water rudders. They could also be fitted with the 50-gallon auxiliary slip tank under the fuselage. Like the Model 35-As, they mounted two 7mm Colt machine guns and A-3 bomb racks under the lower wings, which could accommodate four 116-pound bombs. They did not have radios and, upon delivery, were doped overall aluminum – but most were hastily camouflaged.

The relatively small number of early Model 35-As were the aircraft that bore the brunt of AM action in the far south, but these arrived in small batches in fits-and-starts, amidst a service struggling to cope with both funding and contractual issues with which officials had scant experience.

The Curtiss representative, Joaquin Samper, after the first several aircraft had arrived, been erected, camouflaged, and rushed south, received a telegram around February 18 which read as follows, and which illustrates the highly personalized nature of all of these transactions:

DISCUSSED ADDITIONAL HAWKS WITH CONSUL TODAY. STOP. IN THEIR OPINION PRICE TOO HIGH. STOP. INFORMED THEM TODAY THAT IF THEY WOULD ORDER ADDITIONAL 15 HAWKS BY FEBRUARY 18 OUR MINIMUM PRICE WOULD BE $26,450 WITH DELIVERY OF ALL BY END OF SEVEN WEEKS. STOP. PLEASE DO UTMOST SECURE CONFIRMATION CONSUL. STOP. REQUESTED INFORMATION REGARDING 10 OSPREYS. STOP. WE TOLD HIM CAN DELIVER FIRST IN 35 DAYS AND ALL WITHIN 65 DAYS. STOP. WHAT ARE CHANCES. END.

The Model 65 Sea Hawk Type IIs were MSNs SH15/11754 to SH20/11759 on S.O. 121 delivered between June 30 and July 3, 1933 (AM serials 811 to 816); SH21/11809 to SH25/11813 delivered between March 2 and March 9, 1934 (AM serials 817 to 822), and SH30/11836 to SH35/11841 received between July 24 and 27, 1934 (AM serials 823 to 828). At least two crashed aircraft were either rebuilt or replaced, and these gained AM serials 801a and 805a.

FAC-824 was a Curtiss Model 65 Sea Hawk II, part of the final batch delivered July 24, 1934. Note the deeper chord of the speed ring and the small size of the national insignia on the underside of the starboard wing, compared to earlier practice. The U.S. instructor, left, had just finished qualifying the four AM pilots on the type.

One final aircraft was also acquired by Colombia but has remained something of an enigma. This was the solitary Model 65-A Hawk Type II-A, a landplane, MSN DH46/11767, which, although allegedly destined for Chile or Bolivia, in fact ended its sojourn in Colombia on March 2, 1935. It had been built in July 1933 as a demonstrator and fitted with a Wright R-1820F-3 Cyclone of 650hp and approved as late as August 15, 1934, for U.S. Experimental category license X-13263, and went to Colombia on S.O. 122.

The Sea Hawks served Colombia well, and the service definitely got its money's worth out of them. By February 1943, of the 30 acquired, 16 remained in first-line service.[2]

More Trainers

In line with Colombian ambitions to train their own crews, while the Fledglings acquired earlier had provided excellent transition mounts for pilots partially trained earlier by the Swiss and French Missions, the Curtiss-Wright team rather pointedly observed that what the Colombians really needed was a purpose-built, *ab initio* category, primary trainer.

Stepping forward once again with nearly the ideal aircraft, Curtiss-Wright supplied six aircraft they billed as "Standard Primary Trainers," but which were in fact CW-16Es, all of which had been delivered shortly after March 15, 1933. These were probably MSNs CW16E-3514 to -3520 and gained AM serials 21 to 26. They also provided good service to the AM and were utilized extensively by the U.S. Mission to give primary training to more than 25 Colombian cadets. At least one of them survived until wrecked September 6, 1944 (FAC-21).

And Then the Falcons

Marketed aggressively by the Curtiss-Wright Export Corporation, and probably rightly so, as the nearly perfect companion to the nimble Sea Hawks, were the Curtiss Falcon landplanes and seaplane Falcons, which the company had customized for Colombian conditions.

Seldom recognized to have consisted of two distinct versions, the first three aircraft on S.O. 118 were MSNs SF1/11726 to SF3/11728, which gained AM serials 112 to 114. They were delivered between May 9 and 11, 1933. Similar in many respects to U.S. Army Air Corps O-39s, they differed principally in the engines (712hp SR-1820F-2s) and rather over-engineered undercarriages. They sported three-blade props which, together with the powerful engines, provided a top speed of 182.37mph (at 2,000 feet and 1,950rpm), only slightly lower than their Sea Hawk escorts. These landplanes were not supplied

The very hard-pressed mechanics which accompanied The Group performed miracles with scant prior knowledge of the often exotic – and complex – Curtiss Cyclone Falcon undercarriage assemblies. This is Chappel, learning as he worked. Most of the Falcons with wheels were based at Cali, where they were used as advanced and conversion trainers. The AM crews regarded them as dangerous, as they had poor spin-recovery characteristics.

The massive Bogotá flyover also included nine Curtiss Cyclone Falcons flown by these airmen. Standing, left to right, are Garcia, Lopez, Bernal, another Bernal (brothers?), Almedia, Garcia and, sitting, Sarasty, E. Garcia, and Moncayo.

While intended to handle rough-surface landings, the robust landing gear of the Curtiss Cyclone Falcons tended to fail in the hands of some of the advanced students. Here, AM 118 awaits recovery somewhere in the bush. The Group mechanics spent the overwhelming majority of their time repairing landing gear at Cali!

with auxiliary, ventral slip tanks but could mount one synchronized 7mm fuselage gun, one more in each lower wing, a similar gun for the observer, or a camera mount. As it turned out, these landplane Falcons served most of their lives as trainers. These aircraft were followed by 20 more aircraft, which, rather confusingly, were all labeled by Curtiss as Float Seaplane Falcons (Cyclone), even though only six of them were actually delivered as floatplanes!

The first six of these were delivered between July 1 and 12, 1933, and were MSNs FSF4/11760 to FSF9/11765, on S.O. 122. They became AM 115 to 120. They mounted the same engines as the first three. The fixed, synchronized fuselage gun (a 7mm Browning M-2) had a Type C-3 sight and 300 rounds, while the same type guns in each lower wing could accommodate a rather surprising 1,200 rounds per gun. The 7mm M-2 for the rear gunner had a Type D-4 Wind Vane sight as well as a C-1 gunsight, and provision for 600 rounds of ammunition in six magazines. There were also two A-3 bomb racks under each lower wing, each of which could mount up to one 116-pound bomb.

Colombia held the Falcons in very high esteem and, as early as May 1934, fearing a renewal of Peruvian hostilities, asked Curtiss to investigate on their behalf the possibility of installing two 37mm

Colombia decided to standardize on the muscular Curtiss Seaplane Falcon and Float Seaplane Falcon (Cyclone) as its standard attack aircraft, and this is almost certainly the first, MSN SF1/11726 with Edo 704 floats. Note the partial cockpit canopy for the pilot and absence of any stabilizing dorsal fin.

cannon – one in each upper wing – with a 30-round magazine for each! These were to have been suspended in specially designed fairings some 18 inches below the lower surface of the upper wings and would have of course required the removal of the 7mm guns in the lower wings, although the synchronized gun could be retained. They also inquired about emplacing a similar cannon in the rear gun pit. The Driggs Ordnance Engineering Company seriously considered this installation, and did a number of studies, but when they met to discuss the installation with Curtiss officials in Buffalo, they probably wisely nixed the idea, on the grounds that, after two or three sorties, the upper wings would probably have been completely out of rig and dangerously overstressed!

While the American Mission personnel were nominally "instructors," the truth is that they frequently flew missions to the zone of conflict. Here, Capitáns Jesse Rothrock (left) and E. B. Nobile get ready to deplane with their suitcase after a trip south. Note the camera port, visible under the left rear fuselage, and the housing for the starboard lower wing gun, just inboard of the A-3 bomb racks, as well as the natural metal auxiliary slip tank.

Although of marginal quality, this Falcon is unusual in displaying what appears to be a much-enlarged ventral fin and, in this instance, the auxiliary slip fuel tank has been camouflaged as well. Showing the flag in the southern provinces was encouraged.

These were followed by six more Float Seaplane Falcons on S.O. 130, delivered between March 21 and April 10, 1934, MSNs FSF11/11803 to FSF16/11808 and became AM 121 to 126.

Finally, at least eight more landplanes were acquired on S.O. 136, FSF29/11828 to FSF36/11835, and arrived after July 23, 1934. Of these, only AM serials 127 to 131 are known, suggesting that three of the aircraft may have been replacements for aircraft lost earlier. The existence of serials 116a and 118a indicate that this was probably true in at least two instances.

It appears that about half of the Falcons were camouflaged, and that they saw exceptionally heavy service – the comfort of having a second set of eyes in the rear pit unquestionably being a morale issue when flying over vast, trackless jungle reaches. By February 1943, 13 of them remained on strength with the FAC, of which six were still operating on floats, mostly based at Cali and Palanquero. Incredibly, 12 of these were still on the Order of Battle for September 11, 1946.

The Colombians, by now accustomed to the Curtiss-Wright presence, and possibly in an effort to secure more advantageous rates, made it known during the midst of the negotiations for the Falcons

About half of the Cyclone Falcons remained on wheels for the entirety of their service, including AM 113, MSN SF2/11727 received in May 1933, seen here instructing at Cali.

A number of the Colombian Falcons were delivered without the sliding canopy and half-frame structure, like AM 130, one of the last batch delivered in July 1934. The sturdy undercarriage was well suited to the mostly sod fields from which the aircraft operated. This aircraft does not appear to have provisions for wing guns, and the tail wheel is of interest.

Curtiss Cyclone Falcon AM 118, MSN FSF7/11763, received in July 1933, and probably a veteran of the combat zone. Note the unusual ventral fin. The camouflage consisted of simply splotching light green and brown paint over the original silver painted surfaces in completely random patterns, with the undersides remaining silver – not blue. The starboard lower wing gun muzzle can just be discerned. The rear, flexible guns were usually only mounted when the aircraft were operating in the Leticia region.

Reminiscent of German WWI-era "lozenge" camouflage, this Curtiss Cyclone Falcon, AM 111a, has two passengers in the rear gunner's pit – one of whom appears to be a *señorita*!

that her emissaries in England had been entertaining British counteroffers for from six to 12 Fairey Fox reconnaissance bombers (which had also been sold to Peru), from six to 12 multipurpose de Havilland D.H.84M Dragons, and six multipurpose, armed Avro 626s. Curtiss, however, played their twin trump cards – almost immediate delivery and excellent after-sales support – and the Colombians placed additional orders with them instead.

Besides the German crews that had served, at least ten serving Cuban Army pilots and crewmen (of 11 who had "volunteered")[3] were contracted to fly for the AM during this period, one of whom was Mayor Francisco Terry. This officer, one of the ranking members of the *Cuerpo de Aviación Ejercito de Cuba* (CAEC) in the early 1930s, had been instrumental in the Cuban Army acquisition of a single, armed Bellanca Model 66-75 Aircruiser, and, possibly acting as an agent for the Delaware manufacturer and extoling the multi-role capabilities of the rugged type, came close to brokering a deal for five Aircruisers for the AM which, the AM requested, they desired to be configured as closely as possible to the essentially similar USAAC C-27A. The deal went sour when Terry's agent's fee was discovered, but he may have had a hand in the subsequent acquisition of the exotic Bellanca Model 77-140s sometime later.

Meanwhile, yet another delayed German shipment arrived in the form of two Dornier Do C2As around April 25, 1933. These exotic and remarkably large aircraft (for being single-engine, parasol monoplanes) were equipped with 740hp Hispano-Suiza 12Nbr engines which, almost from the start, proved to be maintenance headaches, as they were the only engines of this type in the country. These aircraft were Dornier Werke Nrs. 229 and 242 and, immediately after being erected, were issued AM serials 811 and 812. However, someone quickly pointed out that these same numbers had already been issued to extant Curtiss Sea Hawks, so they were re-serialed as AM 851 and 852 by June 19. Oddly, German crews who test flew the aircraft invariably cited them in their *Flugbücher* as type Dornier Do K, which has since caused no end of confusion.

A huge aircraft for a two-seat, single-engine design, the two Dornier Do C2As acquired by the AM in April 1933 were handicapped by their exotic engines, 740hp Hispano-Suiza 12Nbrs, a type not used on any other aircraft in the inventory. On the plus side, they carried 20mm Oerlikons which could, with some exertion, be fired as either a dorsal weapon in the rear pit, or from a large oval aperture from the ventral position.

When the two Dornier Do C2As first arrived, they were serialed 811 and 812 briefly, before it was remembered that these serials had already been used on Sea Hawks. Here, 811 wears an incomplete camouflage scheme on her beaching gear but, more interestingly, is in the sesquiplane configuration, not previously reported!

While the engines of the Do C2As were problematic, the fact that they were equipped with a 20mm Oerlikon cannon in the rear position on a universal mount – capable of being fired, with some exertion, from either the dorsal or ventral position (through a rather large, oval, ventral opening), the AM had high hopes for them as anti-shipping weapons. So far as can be determined, however, they never saw action of any sort. Both survived on the AOB as late as July 8, 1940, but were unserviceable – to no one's surprise – due to their engines.

Suddenly, the AM was the proprietor or was soon to be the owner of more aircraft than it knew what to do with.

The *Aviación Militar* Struts its Stuff

In April 1934, as the tensions with Peru were simmering and the AM was busily receiving and assembling its plethora of aircraft, mainly at Cali and Barranquilla, the government of Dr. Olaya Herrera ordered that the bulk of extant combat aircraft and some 40 of the newer aircraft be ferried to a new station. Marginally operational as early as July 1933, the station – *Base Central de Palanquero*, northwest of Bogotá – afforded excellent, if not somewhat isolated facilities for both fixed-gear and seaplane operations. There, as much for the benefit of the citizens of Colombia as for Peruvian military intelligence, the AM organized the *Primera Revista Aérea* (First Air Review), lining up rows of aircraft, including at least five camouflaged Hawks, on wheel undercarriages and equal numbers of Falcons, Ju 52/3ms, and other types. Significantly, however, only a few of the aircraft on the station actually flew during the review, for the pure and simple reason that the AM only possessed about 25 percent of the qualified pilots necessary to fly its inventory of more than 120 airworthy aircraft! Were it not for 11 Cuban CAEC pilots who had also "volunteered" to fly for Colombia during the emergency, as noted, and most of whom were still awaiting return to their island nation, it is doubtful if even this could have been organized.

A surprise visitor in the midst of the busy training schedule set up by the Americans was Spanish aviator Juan Ignacio Pombo in his British Klemm Eagle II, EC-CBB "Santander" (MSN 108/115), pictured here at Cali. Oddly, his itinerary is painted on the aircraft, even though he still had to traverse Central America to his destination, Mexico City.

Reflecting the jungle environment in which it was an outpost, the insignia of the *Base Aérea Palanquero* featured a float-equipped, heavily armed crocodile. This station was about 90 air miles northwest of Bogotá on the Magdalena River and was one of the premier staging posts during the conflict.

Adopted at the suggestion of the American volunteers, the AM commenced painting base-level insignia on at least the port (left) side of the fuselages of assigned aircraft sometime around 1935 or 1936. This is the insignia for *Base Aérea Madrid* near Bogotá, reflecting the headquarters function.

This crew shortfall was a very carefully guarded state secret. When the AM said a hasty goodbye to the German, Cuban, and several other mercenary crews who had answered the call in their time of need – most of the Germans returning home to assume positions in the clandestine *Luftwaffe* – a new alarm in the *frontera del Sur* (Southern Frontier) in mid-1934 brought home to the AM leadership that perhaps some process for creating an adequate, indigenous, and well-trained cadre for the service, which could field its newfound strength, might be overdue.

To the credit of the AM, they had taken good advice and had an adequate number of capable multipurpose training aircraft on hand. The *Curso de Pilotaje Número 2*, staffed by ten of its own veterans as instructors, at the *Base Aérea de "El Guabito"* at Madrid, enabled the AM to get some 45 aircraft into the air by December 1934 at one time – which may well have been a record for all of Latin America up till then.

But it still wasn't enough. The AM leadership, having benefited greatly from the Curtiss-Wright Export Corporation (and which, itself, had almost certainly ensured its own survival in the depths of the Depression via its cash-on-the-barrel-head sales to Colombia) organized overtures via Curtiss-Wright channels as to the possibility of engaging a dedicated instructional cadre from the highly regarded aeronautical establishment in the United States.

That Colombian Camouflage

As noted frequently throughout this narrative, the AM commenced applying camouflage to aircraft destined for the combat zone from nearly the start of hostilities and is noteworthy at this juncture. This was unquestionably the first time that such a measure was employed in a systematic manner in Latin America.

There can be little question that the scheme selected was strongly influenced by the veteran members of the SCADTA organization – the colors were in fact originated in their hangars at Buenaventura and later at Palanquero – and it does not require extensive examination to conclude that it was at least partially influenced by memories of the classic WWI-era "lozenge" patterns so effectively applied to German and Central Powers aircraft during the Great War. It is clear, however, that the colors selected were those readily available at the SCADTA base. Only one firsthand account of the nature of the colors employed has surfaced.

In February 1969, Maximiliano Garavito, at the time editor of the Spanish-language magazine

Adopted from an earlier insignia painted on at least one of the Consolidated P2Y-1C Commodores, this is the insignia of the mainly flying-boat and seaplane-equipped *Base Aérea Buenaventura* on the southwestern, Pacific coast of Colombia. The station was usually abbreviated as simply "B/Tura" by AM crews.

Curtiss-Wright Arrives in Force, Just as the Dust Settles

Curtiss Cyclone Falcon MSN 111a, displaying what is believed to be the most reliable representation of the camouflage colors worn during the Leticia incident yet published.

The fly-past over Bogotá also included two Curtiss-Wright BT-32 Condors and two Junkers Ju 52/3ms, flown by these officers, from left to right Abono, Concho, Herman, Estavez, and Guitierrez. Note the bomb aimer's panels in the nose of the Condor. The BT-32s and Ju 52/3ms were very much regarded at this point as bomber/transports, rather than the other way around.

Revista Aérea Latinoamericana, in response to an inquiry by the late Peter M. Bowers, reported that he had been stationed at the Curtiss factory as an inspector and that when he returned to Colombia, he saw many of the aircraft still camouflaged. His exact words describing what he recalled are as follows: "These were camouflaged with very high colored paints in red, blue and green, resembling the jungle."

The paints were hand-applied, using large brushes and mops in completely random patterns, and no two were alike. Indeed, wide variations can be found. Some had struts painted as well as flying and control surfaces; some did not. Some wrapped nearly all the way around the fuselage, while others had only the upper extremities of the fuselages painted.

Many well-intentioned artists have attempted to interpret the colors and patterns observed, and at least six completely different conclusions have been published to date. The artist for this monograph, Ted Williams, is believed to have been the first, however, to have employed actual spectral analysis of known, good-quality black-and-white photos, to arrive at the colors and patterns accompanying this volume, and they are believed to be the most accurate thus far released.

Some of the surviving aircraft continued to wear these schemes for a number of years after the conflict, while others were fairly quickly repainted in doped aluminum: leading to yet more confusion. Others, including at least six of the Sea Hawks, were apparently camouflaged in a completely different manner by 1936, being painted a solid color on the upper surfaces (probably a dark green) while remaining doped aluminum on the lower surfaces.

There were some notable exceptions, which have proven difficult to explain. The Junkers F 13s and Ju 52/3ms, known to have flown extensively in the south, apparently never received camouflage at all, which, given their value to the effort, is surprising. The Curtiss-Wright BT-32 Condor IIs, even though arriving after the cessation of hostilities, had their massive floats already camouflaged, suggesting that the AM had every intention of employing them in the combat zone had the call come.

Since no known color sketches actually crafted during the period have surfaced, we may never know with certainty what colors or combinations were employed by the AM.

The *Aviación Militar* Serial Number System

With the astonishing expansion of the AM during the course of the Leticia emergency, a practical means of managing their burgeoning inventory became an issue. The service had, perhaps unwittingly, laid down the basic parameters of the system that was eventually embraced, with the straightforward numeric system that had been in use with the service since its very beginnings.

As aircraft entered the inventory, like or similar types were issued either two-digit (for purely training aircraft), following on from the earlier strict numeric system, or three-digit serials for tactical types. What follows is the known issuances during the duration of the crisis and the "arms race" that persisted well into 1936.

AM Serial Number	Type	MSN	Acquired	Notes
15	Curtiss Fledgling J-2	11726	Sep 31	Cr. 16 Mar 34.
15a	Curtiss Fledgling J-2	T3/11732?	16 Jun 33	S.O. 120; cr. 24 May 34.
16	Curtiss Fledgling J-2	11727	Sep 31	Armed; u/s by 5 Feb 43.
17	Curtiss Fledgling J-2	11728	Sep 31	Armed; i/s Apr 44.
18	Curtiss Fledgling j-2	11729	Sep 31	Armed; u/s by 5 Feb 43.
19	Curtiss Fledgling j-2	T1/11730	13 Jun 33	S.O. 120; flown by a German pilot 2 Jun 34; i/s 5 Feb 43.

Curtiss-Wright Arrives in Force, Just as the Dust Settles

AM Serial Number	Type	MSN	Acquired	Notes
20	Curtiss Fledgling J-2	T2/11731	13 Jun 33	S.O. 120; i/s 5 Feb 43.
21	Curtiss-Wright CW-16E Standard Trainer	16E-3509?	After 15 Mar 33	Cr. 6 Sep 44.
22	Curtiss-Wright CW-16E Standard Trainer	16E-3510?	After 15 Mar 33	
23	Curtiss-Wright CW-16E Standard Trainer	16E-3511?	After 15 Mar 33	Named "*Telegrafo*"; Current 17 Jan 34.
24	Curtiss-Wright CW-16E Standard Trainer	16E-3512?	After 15 Mar 33	Current 7 Aug 33; flown by a German pilot.
25	Curtiss-Wright CW-16E Standard Trainer	16E-3513?	After 15 Mar 33	Cr. 17 Jan 34 taxi accident.
26	Curtiss-Wright CW-16E Standard Trainer	16E-3514?	After 15 Mar 33	
27	[may have been reserved for the aborted Loening C2C purchase]			
28	[may have been reserved for the aborted Loening C2C purchase]			
29	[may have been reserved for the aborted Loening C2C purchase]			
30	Consolidated Model 21 (PT-11C)	37	15 Mar 34	i/s 5 Feb 43.
31	Consolidated Model 21 (PT-11C)	38	15 Mar 34	Cr. 15 Feb 37 but repaired; i/s 5 Feb 43.
32	Consolidated Model 21 (PT-11C)	39	15 Mar 34	Cr. 23 Aug 38; repaired; on strength Feb 43 but damaged.
33	Consolidated Model 21 (PT-11C)	40	15 Mar 34	
34	Consolidated Model 21 (PT-11C)	41	15 Mar 34	Cr. in 1935, reportedly re-serialed as FAC 634 but repaired; i/s 5 Feb 43 as 34!
35	Consolidated Model 21 (PT-11C)	42	15 Mar 34	i/s 5 Feb 43.
36	Consolidated Model 21 (PT-11C)	43	15 Mar 34	w/o before 22 Sep 37.
37	Consolidated Model 21 (PT-11C)	44	15 Mar 34	i/s 5 Feb 43.
38	Consolidated Model 21 (PT-11C)	45	15 Mar 34	i/s 5 Feb 43.
39	Consolidated Model 21 (PT-11C)	46	15 Mar 34	i/s 5 Feb 43.
40	Consolidated Model 21 (PT-11C)	47	15 Mar 34	i/s 5 Feb 43.
41	Consolidated Model 21 (PT-11C)	48	15 Mar 34	w/o before 22 Sep 37.
42	Consolidated Model 21 (PT-11C)	49	15 Mar 34	i/s 5 Feb 43.
43	Consolidated Model 21 (PT-11C)	50	15 Mar 34	On strength 5 Feb 43 but under repair.
44	Consolidated Model 21 (PT-11C)	51	15 Mar 34	i/s 5 Feb 43.
45	Consolidated Model 21 (PT-11C)	52	15 Mar 34	To be reduced and salvaged by 5 Feb 43.

AM Serial Number	Type	MSN	Acquired	Notes
46	Consolidated Model 21 (PT-11C)	53	15 Mar 34	i/s 5 Feb 43.
47	Consolidated Model 21 (PT-11C)	54	15 Mar 34	i/s 5 Feb 43.
48	Consolidated (Fleet) Husky 14 (Fleet 2 highly modified)	33	16 Nov 34	Formerly X-524; fate unknown.
49	[untraced]			
50	Fairchild Model 22-C7F	1703	9 May 34	Formerly -14303; cr. 7 Nov 40.
51	Fairchild Model 22-C7F	1704	9 May 34	Formerly -14304; cr. 16 Aug 35.
52	Fairchild Model 22-C7F	1705	9 May 34	Formerly -14305; i/s 5 Feb 43.
101	Wild-Comte X	5	17 Sep 28	i/s 12 Jan 31; re-engined.
102	Wild-Comte X	6	6 May 28	Cr. 20 Oct 29.
103	Wild-Comte X	7	29 Oct 28	i/s 15 Jan 33; re-engined.
104	Wild-Comte X	8	29 Oct 28	i/s 1931.
105	Wild-Comte X	9	6 Nov 28	Cr. at Madrid AB 17 Apr 34; re-engined.
106	Wild-Comte X	10	7 Nov 28	i/s 1932; re-engined.
107	Wild-Comte X	11	9 Nov 28	i/s 12 Jan 31.
108	Wild-Comte X	12	5 Apr 29	Cr. 17 Dec 32 on Caquetá River?
109	Curtiss D-12 Falcon	10877	Mar 28	"*Ricaurte*" but also reported as 111 (q.v.).
110	[untraced]			
111	Curtiss D-12 Falcon	10877	Mar 28	"*Ricaurte*" but also reported as having been 109; camouflaged; armed; lost 18 Feb 33.
111a	Curtiss Cyclone Falcon		Aug 34	Possibly MSN FSF34/11833; seaplane at 5 Feb 43.
112	Curtiss Cyclone Falcon	SF1/11726	9 May 33	S.O. 118; i/s 5 Feb 43 as landplane.
113	Curtiss Cyclone Falcon	SF2/11727	9 May 33	S.O. 118; u/s by Feb 43 as landplane.
114	Curtiss Cyclone Falcon	SF3/11728	11 May 33	S.O. 118; u/s by Feb 43 as landplane.
115	Curtiss Cyclone Falcon	FSF4/11760	1 Jul 33	S.O. 122; w/o before 30 Jan 43.
116	Curtiss Cyclone Falcon	FSF5/11761	1 Jul 33	S.O. 122; cr. 1934.
116a	Curtiss Cyclone Falcon			Possibly MSN FSF35/11834, S.O. 136.; u/s by Feb 43 as seaplane.

AM Serial Number	Type	MSN	Acquired	Notes
117	Curtiss Cyclone Falcon	FSF6/11762	1 Jul 33	S.O. 122; i/s 26 Oct 38; flown by a German pilot 11 Aug 33.
118	Curtiss Cyclone Falcon	FSF7/11763	1 Jul 33	S.O. 122; cr. Sep 34; was flown by a German pilot 14 Aug 33.
118a	Curtiss Cyclone Falcon			Possibly FSF36/11835; cr. 31 Jan 36.
119	Curtiss Cyclone Falcon	FSF8/11764	1 Jul 33	S.O. 122; cr. 7 Aug 38.
120	Curtiss Cyclone Falcon	FSF9/11765	12 Jul 33	S.O. 122; i/s 5 Feb 43 as seaplane.
121(1)	Curtiss-Wright C14R Osprey	C14R-2017?	Dec 32	i/s 23 Mar 33; i/s 3 Jul 39 but being overhauled.
121(2)	Curtiss Cyclone Falcon	FSF11/11803	21 Mar 34	S.O. 130; i/s 5 Feb 43 as seaplane.
122(1)	Curtiss-Wright C14R Osprey	C14R-2018?	Dec 32	Possibly the one lost at Flandes 8 Feb 33 on floats.
122(2)	Curtiss Cyclone Falcon	FSF12/11804	21 Mar 34	S.O. 130; cr. 28 Apr 38.
123(1)	Curtiss-Wright C14R Osprey	C14R-2016?	Dec 32	Collided with CW-16E "25" in 1934.
123(2)	Curtiss Cyclone Falcon	FSF13/11805	21 Mar 34	S.O. 130; u/s by Feb 43 as landplane.
124	Curtiss Cyclone Falcon	FSF14/11806	21 Mar 34	S.O. 130; i/s 5 Feb 43 as seaplane.
125	Curtiss Cyclone Falcon	FSF15/11807	21 Mar 34	S.O. 130; u/s by Feb 43 as landplane but had been a seaplane at one point.
126	Curtiss Cyclone Falcon	FSF16/11808	10 Apr 34	S.O. 130; i/s by 5 Feb 43 as seaplane.
127	Curtiss Cyclone Falcon	FSF29/11828	23 Jul 34	S.O. 136; cr. 3 Jan 35.
128	Curtiss Cyclone Falcon	FSF30/11829	23 Jul 34	S.O. 136; cr. 22 Apr 43 at sea as seaplane.
129	Curtiss Cyclone Falcon	FSF31/11830	23 Jul 34	S.O. 130; but reported in service 15 Mar 33!
130	Curtiss Cyclone Falcon	FSF32/11831	23 Jul 34	u/s by Feb 43 as landplane.
131	Curtiss Cyclone Falcon	FSF33/11832	23 Jul 34	S.O. 136; cr. 22 Mar 35.
181	Seversky SEV-3M-WW	3(37)	Jul 36	Tested as NX-15391; u/s by 5 Feb 43.
182	Seversky SEV-3M-WW	4(38)	Jul 36	Tested as NX-15689; u/s by 5 Feb 43.
183	Seversky SEV-3M-WW	5(39)	Jul 36	Tested as NX-15928; w/o 30 Apr 37 at Madrid, two killed.

AM Serial Number	Type	MSN	Acquired	Notes
201	Junkers F 13	758	1932	Ex-SCADTA A-21, C-21; re-serialed as PF-1; wfu 1939.
201	Junkers W 33	2719	Sep 32	Ex-SCADTA A-33 and C-33; to 404.
202	Junkers F 13	543	9 Sep 32	Ex-D-152, Dz-35, SCADTA A-18, C-18, C-38; w/o 21 May 33; but also cited as MSN 771 ex-C-18; armed; lost on the Putumayo in 1933.
203	Junkers F 13	2009	9 Sep 32	Ex-SCADTA C-25; to PF-2; but also cited as MSN 758 ex-C-21; wfu 1939.
205	Hamilton H45/47	58	17 Feb 33	Formerly NC-466E; floats and named "*Aguila II*"; not reported after 17 May 33.
401	Junkers K 43do	2571	Nov 32	P&W Wasp S3H1; floats.
402	Junkers K 43do	2572	Nov 32	P&W Wasp S3H1; i/s 2 May 46.
403	Junkers K 43do	2573	Sep 33	Floats; i/s Mar 42.
404(1)	Junkers W 33	2719		Formerly SCADTA A-33 and C-33, and AM 201(2); modified and armed; floats; still in service 11 Sep 46.
404(2)	Junkers W 34h	2817	Jun 34	P&W Hornet T2D1; floats; i/s Mar 42.
405	Junkers W 34h	2818	Jun 34	
405a	Junkers W 34hi	2831?	20 Jul 40	Ex-SCADTA? Floats; i/s Mar 42.
406	Junkers W 34L/h	2819	Jun 34	i/s 19 Feb 40.
406a	Junkers W 34hi	2833	1942	Ex-SCADTA? P&W Wasp S3H1G; floats; i/s Mar 42 but under repair.
407	Junkers W 34h	2823	Sep 34	P&W Hornet T2D1; purported to be the aircraft in the FAC museum now; wfu 1942.
408	Junkers W 34L/h	2824	Sep 34	w/o Jun 41.
408a	Junkers W 34hi	2835	1942	Ex-SCADTA? P&W Wasp C; floats; under repair Mar 42.

AM Serial Number	Type	MSN	Acquired	Notes
409	Junkers W 34h	2825	Sep 34	P&W Hornet T2d1; floats; u/s by 16 Dec 37 but returned to service by Mar 42.
601	Dornier Wal (passenger)	81(61)	Sep 32	Formerly I-AZDD, SCADTA C-28; i/s 11 Sep 46.
602[4]	Dornier Do J Wal IId			On hand as early as 17 Apr 33.
603	Dornier Do J Wal IId	221(34)	12 Jan 33	P&W S3H1 engines; force-landed into trees 25 Nov 34 but reported i/s 5 Feb 43.
604	Dornier Do J Wal IId	222(35)	12 Jan 33	P&W S3H1 engines; reported wfu in 1947.
611	Consolidated P2Y-1C	1	28 Dec 32	Formerly X-2101; i/s 11 Sep 46.
612	Consolidated P2Y-1C			
613	[apparently not used]			
614	Consolidated P2Y-1C		27 Apr 33	Flown by a German pilot.
621	Junkers Ju 52/3mde	4010	Apr 33	Floats and later wheels; u/s by 5 Feb 43.
622	Junkers Ju 52/3mde	4011	Apr 33	Floats and later wheels; i/s 1948.
623	Junkers Ju 52/3mde	4012	4 May 34	Formerly D-9; w/o at Cabuyaro 18 Feb 35.
624	Junkers Ju 52/3mg4e	4031	May 34	Floats and later wheels; w/o 14 (or 16) Jan 36, 20 minutes after take-off from Puerto Boy en route to Tres Esquinas, 14 killed; overloaded.
625	Junkers Ju 52/3mg4e	4032	Mar 34	Wheels only; briefly assigned as presidential aircraft with a red band around the rear fuselage; to the FAC Museum.
626	Junkers Ju 52/3mg4e	4034	Mar 34	Floats and later wheels; i/s 5 Feb 43; wfu 1950.
641	Ford Model 5-AT-B	5-AT-44	17 Feb 36	Formerly NC-9687/"2"; cr. 21 Apr 41 but repaired as i/s 26 Sep 45.
642	Ford Model 5-AT-C	5-AT-89	7 Nov 35	Formerly NC-429H; reported w/o 15 Aug 41 but also cited to AN-AAD.

AM Serial Number	Type	MSN	Acquired	Notes
643	Ford Model 5-AT-C	5-AT-47	17 Feb 36	Formerly NC-9690/"3"; cr. 22 Apr 41 but repaired; operated on floats; to HC-SBK?
644	Ford Model 5-AT-C	5-AT-67	17 Feb 36	Formerly NC-408H; cr. 27 Aug 41 between Tarapaca and La Pedrera.
645	Ford Model 5-AT			Unconfirmed, but reported w/o before 30 Jan 43; possibly an ex-SCADTA aircraft.
651	Curtiss-Wright BT-32 Condor II	54	1 Jun 34	On floats; i/s 24 Jan 44.
652	Curtiss-Wright BT-32 Condor II	55	18 Jun 34	Scrapped after 11 Sep 46.
653	Curtiss-Wright BT-32 Condor II	56	24 Jun 34	Dbf at San José del Guaviare 31 Jan 42.
671	Bellanca Model 77-140	1201	Feb 36	i/s 18 Mar 40.
672	Bellanca Model 77-140	1203	Feb 36	
673	Bellanca Model 77-140	1202	Sep 38	
674	Bellanca Model 77-140	1204	Sep 38	
***	Curtiss Model 35-A Sea Hawk Type I	SH1/11653	31 Oct 32	S.O. 110; apparently wrecked during tests and never serialed.
801	Curtiss Model 35-A Sea Hawk Type I	SH2/11654	31 Oct 32	S.O. 110; cr. 15 Feb 33 while being flown by German Cpt. Brethfield – hit a log in the water while attempting to take off at Barrancabermeja; aircraft sunk.
801a	Curtiss Model 65-A Sea Hawk Type II-A	DH46/11767	2 Mar 35	Not confirmed link. S.O. 122; originally earmarked for Bolivia via Chile; a landplane, it was under repair by 5 Feb 43.
802	Curtiss Model 35-A Sea Hawk Type I	SH3/11655	7 Nov 32	S.O. 110; w/o before 30 Jan 43.
803	Curtiss Model 35-A Sea Hawk Type I	SH4/11656	7 Nov 32	S.O. 110; cr. 15 Jul 41 and again 23 Aug 43, as a landplane, into a home in the center of the city of Honda; w/o.
804	Curtiss Model 35-A Sea Hawk Type I	SH5/11657	27 Dec 32	S.O. 112; i/s Feb 43 but under repair; landplane.
805	Curtiss Model 35-A Sea Hawk Type I	SH6/11658	9 Jan 33	S.O. 112. w/o before Aug 33.

Curtiss-Wright Arrives in Force, Just as the Dust Settles

AM Serial Number	Type	MSN	Acquired	Notes
805a	Curtiss Model ??-? Sea Hawk		Aug 33	In service by 1934 but there is no known Curtiss MSN to match this replacement. It may have been built-up locally from two aircraft. Under repair by 5 Feb 43 as a landplane.
806	Curtiss Model 35-A Sea Hawk Type I	SH10/11701	14 Mar 33	S.O. 117; cr. 25 Apr 40.
807	Curtiss Model 35-A Sea Hawk Type I	SH11/11702	14 Mar 33	S.O. 117; i/s circa 1945.
808	Curtiss Model 35-A Sea Hawk Type I	SH12/11703	14 Mar 33	S.O. 117; cr. 15 Jul 41 but repaired, as i/s Feb 43 but under repair, as a landplane.
809	Curtiss Model 35-A Sea Hawk Type I	SH13/11704	14 Mar 33	S.O. 117; i/s 1945; under repair as a landplane by 5 Feb 43.
810	Curtiss Model 35-A Sea Hawk Type I	SH14/11705	24 Mar 33	S.O. 117; i/s 1945; under repair 5 Feb 43 as a landplane.
811(1)	Dornier Do C2A	229	8 May 33	Sesquiplane; re-serialed 851 by 24 Jun 33.
811(2)	Curtiss Model 65 Sea Hawk II	SH15/11754	30 Jun 33	S.O. 121; i/s Jun 43 but under repair as a landplane.
812(1)	Dornier Do c2A	242	25 Apr 33	Parasol monoplane; re-serialed 852 by 19 Jun 33.
812(2)	Curtiss Model 65 Sea Hawk II	SH16/11755	30 Jun 33	S.O. 121; cr. 5 Jan 39.
813	Curtiss Model 65 Sea Hawk II	SH17/11756	30 Jun 33	S.O. 121; i/s Jun 43 on floats.
814	Curtiss Model 65 Sea Hawk II	SH18/11757	30 Jun 33	S.O. 121; i/s 1945 on floats; had been damaged by 5 Feb 43, at which time it was a landplane.
815	Curtiss Model 65 Sea Hawk II	SH19/11758	30 Jun 33	S.O. 121; w/o before 30 Jan 43, possibly in 1936.
816	Curtiss Model 65 Sea Hawk II	SH20/11759	3 Jul 33	S.O. 121; w/o before 30 Jan 43.
817	Curtiss Model 65 Sea Hawk II	SH21/11809	2 Mar 34	S.O. 129; i/s Jan 43 as a floatplane.
818	Curtiss Model 65 Sea Hawk II	SH22/11810	2 Mar 34	S.O. 129; cr. 15 Jul 41.
819	Curtiss Model 65 Sea Hawk II	SH23/11811	2 Mar 34	S.O. 129; i/s Jun 43 as a floatplane.

AM Serial Number	Type	MSN	Acquired	Notes
820	Curtiss Model 65 Sea Hawk II	SH24/11812	2 Mar 34	S.O. 129; w/o 25 May 42 at Madrid AB; rough landing or take-off tore the engine from the aircraft; destroyed by fire. This same aircraft was reported wrecked 24 Jul 38 while performing in front of the President, killing 65 spectators on the ground!
821	Curtiss Model 65 Sea Hawk II	SH25/11813	2 Mar 34	S.O. 129; i/s 5 Feb 43 as a floatplane.
822	Curtiss Model 65 Sea Hawk II	SH26/11814	9 Mar 34	S.O. 129; w/o on landing at Palanquero 8 Aug 43; landplane.
823	Curtiss Model 65 Sea Hawk II	SH30/11836	24 Jul 34	S.O. 135; cr. 19 Nov 43.
824	Curtiss Model 65 Sea Hawk II	SH31/11837	24 Jul 34	S.O. 135; w/o before 30 Jan 43; landplane.
825	Curtiss Model 65 Sea Hawk II	SH32/11838	24 Jul 34	S.O. 135; i/s Feb 43, landplane.
826	Curtiss Model 65 Sea Hawk II	SH33/11839	24 Jul 34	S.O. 135; w/o before 30 Jan 43.
827	Curtiss Model 65 Sea Hawk II	SH34/11840	24 Jul 34	S.O. 135; w/o before 30 Jan 43.
828	Curtiss Model 65 Sea Hawk II	SH35/11841	27 Jul 34	S.O. 135; w/o before 30 Jan 43.
851	Dornier Do c2A	229	24 Jun 33	Formerly AM 811 briefly; i/s 8 Jul 40.
852	Dornier Do c2A	242	19 Jun 33	Formerly AM 812 briefly; i/s by 8 Jul 40.
900	Junkers W 34h	2827	Jan 35	i/s 1 Jan 50.

cr. – crashed; S.O. – sales order; u/s – unserviceable; i/s – in service; w/o – written off; wfu – withdrawn from use; dbf – destroyed by fire

Chapter 6
El Misión de Aviación Norteamericana

So important had Colombia become to the Curtiss fortunes that, in mid-March 1933, George Chapline, Director of Sales and Service for the Corporation, arrived in person at Barranquilla aboard the S.S. *Colombia* – a vessel which was destined to figure prominently in the travels of many aviators and subsequent shipments of aircraft, parts, and spares – to evaluate any additional opportunities in the country. As a secondary mission, he saw to arrangements for the arrival of shipments already "in the pipeline" as well as some lingering cost negotiations.

Seldom noted, Curtiss-Wright had actually contracted for none other than the highly efficient SCADTA organization, as described earlier, to receive and, in most instances, actually assemble

One of the tasks set before the Mission was to organize a huge fly-past over the capital city, Bogotá, not long after their arrival. The ten pilots shown here all flew Consolidated PT-11Cs during that event. They are standing, left to right, Olano, Gonzalez, Posada, Rocha, Duarte, Pinto and, sitting, Valdes, Correa, Nieto, and Arango. Note Ju 52/3m MSN 625 in the background which, by this time, had a red band around the rear fuselage adjoining the serial.

the growing number of aircraft types arriving bound for the AM, all under the direction of a small Curtiss team.

What rapidly became very apparent, however, was the growing realization that, with the impending departure of the Germans, Cubans, and others, the AM's training establishment simply could not meet the needs of the service – an appreciation that Curtiss and the AM leadership appear to have reached independently.

Thus, from late 1933, through the "hangar grapevine" in the United States, where any hint of a job opportunity in the field was eagerly seized upon during the depths of the Depression – as well as more formal channels – the word slowly spread that "Colombia was hiring," not only pilots, but mechanics familiar with Curtiss aircraft as well – and that she was willing to pay rather handsomely.

This clarion call came at a very propitious moment for many. The nearly concurrent cancellation of all existing air mail contracts in the U.S. in February 1934 had thrown a host of experienced pilots and crews out of work in the midst of a very hard winter. The U.S. Army Air Corps itself, struggling to cope with increasingly stringent budgetary restraints, which limited its commissioned pilot strength at a time when extraordinary demands were being made upon it, had turned to the expedient of training and commissioning reserve officers – then "using them up" until funding and their temporary active duty tours expired.

And so it developed that most of the crews and "wrenches" who signed up for the exotic allure of Colombia migrated from these two groups, with the majority being ex-service Reservists.

Second Lieutenant Franklin K. Paul, Air Reserve, writing in a letter dated February 7, 1934, from his posting at Langley Field, Virginia, to the Department of Commerce and Department of State, asked point-blank if "the rumor that Colombia is hiring pilots" was true. Officials at the Department of Commerce replied to this – and numerous similar letters – by stating that it had "no objections…to such activity during time of peace," but that it was "not looked upon with favor during a time of war."

Legally, Peru and Colombia were not at war, although the bullets, bombs, and shells that had been exchanged were real enough, as were the known casualties. And so, it was this strict and "official" definition that led more than 25[1] U.S. nationals to answer Colombia's call.

All volunteers, they were, unbeknownst at the time, the first American Volunteer Group. A similar organization would emerge in China within seven years.

More Aircraft Arrive

Although it hadn't been planned that way, the arrival of the first of 18 sturdy Consolidated PT-11Cs, in March 1934, coincided with the expanded AM training program brilliantly. These aircraft, although marketed as "primary trainers," were in fact multipurpose types capable of being mounted on twin floats and with modest armament fittings – no guns, but A-3 bomb racks under the center line. There is no record of them being employed in this role, however.

The PT-11Cs were MSNs 37 to 54 and received AM serials 30 to 47. These were among some of the first AM aircraft to start receiving the new station emblems, which had been suggested by members of the U.S. mission as a morale and *esprit de corps* measure. Incredibly, five of these aircraft survived countless indignities to remain on the FAC Air Order of Battle as late as December 2, 1952! Only nine PT-11Cs are known to have suffered accidents, and of these, at least two were repaired, while three were complete write-offs, and two collided in flight on February 18, 1937.

So, it transpired that, against the backdrop of all that has been described to this point, on April 12, 1934, in the words of one of their leaders, Major J. H. "Jesse" Rothrock, USAAC (Res.), "58 pilots, mechanics, a wife, one Mother-in-Law and two dogs"[2] set sail from New York aboard the S.S. *Colombia* bound for Cartagena on the Colombian northern Caribbean coast.

The very first Consolidated PT-11C, AM 30 (MSN 37) had arrived in March 1934 but by the time this image was taken at Cali had apparently sprung the main gear somewhat, as she is exhibiting a decided list to starboard! The AM carried individual aircraft serials under the inner port wings, upper right, and both sides of the fuselage, and on the PT-11Cs, the serials were also repeated in smaller numerals at the top of the vertical fins. These 18 aircraft were almost perfect for conditions in Colombia.

AM Consolidated PT-11C MSN 44 (MSN 51) as she appeared shortly after arrival. This aircraft was still in daily use as late as February 5, 1943. The PT-11Cs were heavily engaged by the instructors of the U.S. Mission as they gave tuition to some of Colombia's best and brightest – many of whom, as of 1934, had not even learned to drive a car.

Oddly enough, this rather noisy and transparent expedition excited very little press commentary, with only one known 6-inch story in the *New York Times* supplying a dock-side account. Not a single mention of the expedition could be located in any of the multitude of normally comprehensive aviation journals of the day, save *Interavia No. 109*, which devoted a single paragraph, including details of the compensation expected.

When The Group first arrived, an "additional duty" that the Colombians asked them to perform was to recover and rebuild this Consolidated PT-11C (almost certainly MSN 34, MSN 41) from the Rio Cauca, where it had been submerged for ten months after hitting a ferry cable during a practice force-landing. Surveying the mess is John Hayden and German Olano. They succeeded in doing so, but, in the words of one of the members, "it was never quite right again."

PT-11C AM 32 was the third example to be erected and tested by the U.S. Mission, and in this case, also carried her individual serial number on the mid-fuselage side as well.

The *Times* article did speculate, however, that they sailed "in defiance of an official government protest," which, as will be seen, must have been merely a *pro forma* gesture, since the U.S. government had, indirectly, aided in the financing for the fleet of Curtiss and Curtiss-Wright aircraft,[3] as well as probably some of the others, and unofficially regarded Colombia as the "injured" party in regards to Leticia.

Additionally, and although no written document has been found making mention of the circumstances, the fact that the Germans, via their invaluable SCADTA organization, had achieved nearly complete control of the AM must not have escaped the attentions of U.S. intelligence services charged with defense of the nearby Panama Canal. Thus, even an "informal" U.S. mission, comprised of mainly USAAC Reserve officers, or former officers, must have presented a far more appealing scenario, and these elements may well have "greased the wheels" for the participants.

The Group also included, in the beginning at least, some "big name" participants. None other than Bernt Balchen, Admiral Byrd's pilot during the famous South Pole flights, was linked to the group, but no evidence has been located substantiating the *Times* claim that he was a leader of what came to be known as "The American Group" or, simply, "The Group."

Likewise, Clyde Pangborn, he of the first non-stop Pacific flight, was also a participant, which was at least partially correct: he *was* indeed traveling to Cartagena on the same ship, but *only* as the Fairchild Aircraft Company's representative, which was attempting – with limited success – to get in on the lucrative Colombian business (he in fact succeeded in selling only the noted trio of Fairchild Model 22 C7Fs to the AM, and these at a bargain price, in the hope of follow-up orders).

Most of the pilots in The Group volunteered the information that they would draw between $350 and $500 per month, depending on duty assignment, but insisted that contracts would be terminated

Three of these unusual parasol Fairchild Model 22 C7Fs arrived May 9, 1934, and AM 50 was MSN 1703. Favored for aerobatic work, one survived until November 1946.

Although Curtiss-Wright had secured orders for as many as 12 multi-purpose A14R Ospreys, only three are known to have entered service around December 1932 – serials 121, 122 and 123. Although one was mounted on twin floats (two sets had been ordered), 123 suffered a catastrophic ground collision with CW-16 number 25 in 1934 while on standard wheel undercarriage (as shown here). The A14Rs, ironically, would have provided ideal mounts for the combats actually experienced on the Putumayo with Peruvian aircraft.

"immediately upon any declaration of war," although reports persisted that they were intended to fly actively – not just as instructor cadre – for the AM, and that they would "get a bonus for each Peruvian machine brought down."

The "war bride" in the party, the former Jeannette Penn of Hempstead, Long Island, New York, who married James McLeod only two days prior to sailing, was aboard the ship on April 12 and, contrary to Major Rothrock's accounting, several other fliers reportedly arranged to have their families travel to Colombia as well, some following later – several even flying down via Pan Am, a genuine extravagance at the time.

Initially, the members of The Group were signed to six-month contracts, with pilots receiving $500 per month and mechanics $200 to $250 per month, plus unidentified "expenses" – probably uniforms. These were princely sums during the Depression. One member, John L. "Sunny" Trunk, who was generally regarded to have been more willing to talk to newsmen than others, insisted that the agreements called only for instruction services and that in case of war, "everything was off." Trunk emerged as the ranking member of The Group in Colombia, as it unfolded.[4]

It appears, however, that at least some of the pilots – most likely those with tactical aircraft experience – were secretly contracted on a contingency basis for "war services" as well, and the matter of "kill" bonuses was informally but significantly discussed, according to Jesse Rothrock, one of the principal pilots and officers of The Group.

At any rate, upon arrival at Cartagena, the pilots were almost immediately checked out on the fleet of float-equipped Curtiss Sea Hawks and Falcons that had been assembled there by SCADTA crews by a Curtiss-employed pilot who has eluded identification, as noted earlier in this account. The Group stayed at Cartagena a little less than five months while diplomatic wrangling continued, and meanwhile trained on the Curtiss equipment for events which might develop – a "force in being" – certainly not uncounted in the deliberations with the Peruvian opposition and mediators.

Above left: Usually cited as "the two Jefes," at left is Colombian Mayor Ernesto Buenaventura, commander of the *Base Central de Palanquero* and the de facto leader of the American mission, Capitán John H. L. Trunk, wearing his new Colombian rank insignia on his epaulettes.

Above right: Pursuit instructors near the "ready room" having a smoke before demonstrating proper procedure. From left to right, Trunk, Nobile, Peenstra, and Hayden. Note the Hawk near the shack has no serial number.

Military access documents seem to be a universal norm, and this ID pass was issued to Jesse Rothrock to allow him unfettered access to the AM base at Cartagena while the Americans were assembling the Curtiss fleet.

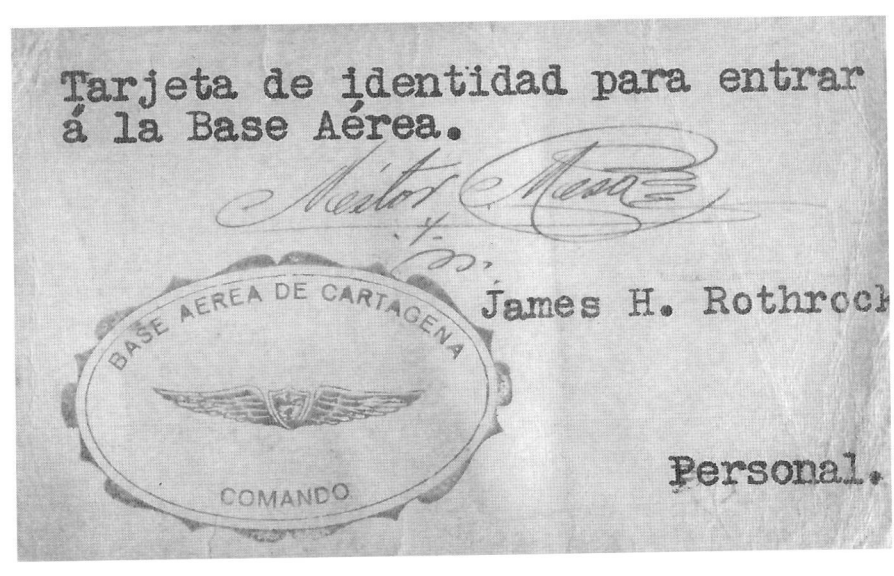

The Group then transferred, in flights of four and five aircraft (with the rest of the crews flown out on board Condor and Ju 52 transports) to the newly expanded base at Palanquero, on the Magdalena north of Hondo, a site not found on most maps, then or now. There, about half of the aircraft were converted back to wheel undercarriages (much to the relief of members of The Group, few of whom had much seaplane experience) and then flown on to Cali where, following the success of diplomacy, The Group actually launched a very well-organized training center for Colombian cadets and ground crews, just as advertised.

Possibly the first Americans to ever fly aboard German-piloted Ju 52/3ms, seen here are most of the members of the "American Mission" in front of AM 621 at Cartagena in July 1934. From left to right, they are Terrell, Patterson, Brewster, Haley, Mayor Terry (a Cuban Army pilot), Wackowitz, Jesse Rothrock, Chappel, and Kent.

During their five-month sojourn at Palanquero, most of the single members of The Group found quarters aboard this vessel, tied up just above the seaplane ramps.

Patterned after curricula gleaned in whole or in part from their own experiences in the USAAC training establishment, the *Norte Americanos*, who had gained respect for the Germans of SCADTA and the Colombian cadre of the AM, soon found themselves in charge of the entire program.

Although the Americans admired the rugged German equipment, personnel, and efficiency, they didn't think much of their training methods which, while probably adequate in Germany, where Teutonic influences prevailed, often didn't suit Latin American conditions or, specifically, Colombian etiquette. The Germans, for instance, had instituted the prevailing European system for control of the landing area at Cali that, essentially, amounted to a lowly "*soldado*" (private) at the end of a landing area more or less favoring the prevailing winds, with a red and green flag. Waving red at an aircraft running straight-in for landing meant "go around again," while green, of course, meant proceed "at your own risk!"

The Americans quickly replaced this system with the typical U.S. left-hand, counterclockwise pattern around a specified landing area, a novelty for the Colombians, but one which they quickly found more efficient, safe, and practical.

The Group members had nearly all agreed to have their monthly pay, the contracts for which were extended, for most of the 58 members, to a full 18 months, deposited in a New York bank in U.S. currency.

Above left: The flying attire of the instructors was often a mix of German, U.S., and Colombian gear, and the Americans were suspicious of the parachutes the AM produced for them, of unknown provenance! This is Nobile, one of the leading members of The Group.

Above right: The mobile "ready room" at Cali was rather primitive but functional. Note the flag held by the officer in the foreground, soon to be dispensed with, and the cattle skull adorning the peak of the roof!

Above left: Here, Bubeck and Lundy sport USAAC trousers, belts, and belt-buckles, with rather casual tropical shirts beside one of the instructional Curtiss Cyclone Falcons at Cali, which boasted a concrete hard-standing.

Above right: Seven officer members of The Group, from left to right: a rather rumpled Jesse Rothrock, Haley, Woodward, Nobile, Trunk, Hayden, and Herman, at Cali August 9, 1934. While their uniforms and headgear were AM issue, two of the pilots wear USAAC wings.

However, as more and more Colombians became graduates, and as the border tensions gradually melted away, the Colombians moved to pay the members in local *peso* currency, which did not sit well with the vast majority of the members of The Group.

In fact, it was this move which resulted in the virtual dissolution of The Group, as such, by September 1935, leaving only seven senior members. These were one "Jefe" (who held the assimilated rank of *Capitán* in the AM, complete with uniform), at $500 per month, and six *Tenientes*, each drawing $350 per month. They were joined by nine mechanics and three radio operators. By January 6, 1937, this number had been slowly eroded, and only three remained (John L. Trunk, Chief Instructor at the *Escuela Militar* "Ernesto Samper," John H. Hayden, a Ford instructor and pilot, and O. K. Haley, a senior flight instructor). Ironically, they had by then been joined by a German, Major Rolf Starke, who was the Chief Technical Advisor to the Headquarters of the AM (apparently serving from February 1, 1935, through March 31, 1937, at $500 per month) and Cpt. Waldemar Roeder, who specialized in Junkers aircraft, who served from April 1, 1936, through March 31, 1938, at $420 per month.

Some of the pilots and mechanics who, for the most part, had enjoyed their Colombian sojourn, elected to stay on, some to work for SCADTA or other emerging aviation enterprises, but most returned to the U.S., with a tidy bankroll, to face a slowly recovering America.

Despite intensive research, no complete roster of the original 58 members has been located and, their protests notwithstanding, at least two – and probably many more – are known to have made excursions in camouflaged, armed combat aircraft to the distant *Zona del Sur*. Clearly, the majority were former USAAC members with a sprinkling of former commercial pilots (especially some with Ford Tri-motor ratings). Oddly, only one U.S. Navy airman has been identified (a Lieutenant E. B. Nobile, who held a USN (Reserve) commission), aside from a strange note found in the U.S. Senate Hearings on Arms Trafficking, which noted that, as of February 8, 1934, a Commander James Strong, USN, had resigned his

El Misión de Aviación Norteamericana

And the real reason for the presence of the U.S. Mission, the next generation of AM pilots, "*Los Alumnos*" – who could easily pass for aviation cadets anywhere as of 1935. From left to right, they were Velez, Arango, Valdés, Piñeros, Ibarguen, Tellez, and Rocha. They were among Colombia's best and brightest.

One of the more mysterious of the U.S. pilots who eventually became a member of the Mission, Capitán E. B. Nobile had been one of at least two North Americans to serve in combat. Here, he stands amidst the misery that was the Leticia zone with a local mascot.

Above left: Although he flew Model 35-A Sea Hawk Type Is for the most part – one of the few pilots in the country to have experience on Curtiss aircraft – he specialized in flying the Falcons and is pictured here, probably at Palanquero, complete with pistol and machete sidearms, after just returning from the Zone. Note the auxiliary slip fuel tank and underwing bomb rack.

Above right: At least three wives were known to have ultimately accompanied their American husbands to Colombia, including Billie Hayden, John Hayden's better half, who endeared herself to the group as she was the solitary member of the expedition who had any Spanish language ability whatsoever!

commission to take an advisory role for the AM – and which testimony claimed he had been designated as the commanding officer of the AM! Not a solitary member of The Group recalled any such person.

Although the training regimen that The Group established proved to be very effective, not a single word has come to light regarding any language difficulties, although such must surely have existed, at least in the beginning. One participant seemed to recall that some of the wives gave occasional English classes, but it appears more likely that some of the serving AM cadre spoke English and acted as interpreters as needed.

Even More Aircraft Arrive

The members of The Group were often informally consulted regarding the continuing aircraft acquisitions that the AM and Colombian government agents seemed determined to continue – undoubtedly due to the excellent commissions that were associated with these deals.

But just as the last of the Curtiss Model 65 Sea Hawks arrived and were being assembled, several of the officers were asked for their opinions of two Dutch aircraft types, specifically the venerable

An otherwise unknown Hawk loss was in June 1934 when American pilot Wackowitz fell out of this aircraft while doing aerobatics over Cartagena bay – without having his seatbelt fastened. He parachuted safely but left the country ahead of the rest of The Group. The engine was not recovered. A camouflaged example, this may have been AM 816.

Fokker C.VE biplane reconnaissance bomber, and the Fokker D.XVIIA fighter. The Americans, quite correctly, denied any knowledge of these types and, when shown the sales brochures and prospectus for a lot of ten each (which gave performance figures in metrics), the members of The Group reportedly expressed the guarded view that they did not seem to offer any improvement over the Sea Hawks and Falcons which were on hand in abundance.

They were excited, however, to learn that the efforts of Clyde Pangborn, representing Fairchild interests, had been modestly successful, and that three brand-new Model 22C7F parasol trainers – which they regarded very highly as a truly "advanced" trainer – were due to arrive on May 9, 1934.

These aircraft, MSNs 1703 to 1705, had actually been built on speculation by Fairchild, and issued U.S. Department of Commerce Identification Numbers 14303 to 14305. These became AM 50 to 52 and, reportedly, were augmented by a fourth aircraft, MSN 1707 (ID No.14343), which was nominally purchased for the infant *Escuela de Aviación Civil*. In fact, it was apparently flown and maintained by The Group and the AM. One of these aircraft was badly damaged November 16, 1937, while being flown by Tte. Bernardo Escobedo, when he was obliged to make a forced landing in a rice field near Cali, but the other two soldiered on as late as May 2, 1946.

Big Orders with Too Much Momentum

At the height of the crisis with Peru, Colombian resolve and wherewithal proved quite remarkable. The leadership in Bogotá had juggled the powerful German and SCADTA interests, significant numbers of foreigners, and cunning salesmen from the United States and elsewhere with finesse, all things being considered.

But several orders, which seemed excellent decisions at the time, simply absorbed more lead-time than had been anticipated – and, in the meantime, bowing to international pressure, hostilities were smothered.

The trio of Curtiss-Wright BT-32 Condor IIs were flight-delivered to Barranquilla via the Pan American base at Dinner Key, Miami, Florida, and the U.S. Naval Air Station Coco Solo, Canal Zone. Here, nose-to-nose at Dinner Key on a special submersible platform, two await their long flights. Note the complete absence of serial numbers of ferry registrations and that the floats have not been camouflaged.

Certainly, one of the most dramatic of these was the order for three Curtiss-Wright BT-32 Condor II bomber/transports, which in fact were unique in being the only aircraft from the Curtiss empire to be flight-delivered to Colombia, other than the very first D-12 Falcon, *Ricaurte*. Flown to Barranquilla via Miami, they arrived one at a time on June 1, 18, and 24, 1934. The three aircraft were all flown to Colombia by the same U.S. pilot: Harry D. Copland, who also checked out AM crews – and members of The Group – on flying the rather intimidating aircraft.

These aircraft had been eagerly sought by Colombia as early as May 1933, when W. F. Goulding, Vice-President of the Curtiss-Wright Export Corporation, received a direct appeal via Colombian General Angel, who advised him that his government very much desired some aircraft "in the heavy bomber category," both of the patrol type, like the P2Y-1Cs that they had recently acquired, and BT-32s which could be operated as both land- and seaplanes.

General Angel did not pull any punches. He told Goulding that Colombia, via Clyde Pangborn, had also approached Bellanca about constructing a heavier, bomber version of the Airbus. This, of course, resulted in the truly exotic Bellanca 77-140 – which Colombia also ordered, and about which more anon.

Goulding immediately pointed out to Angel that the BT-32 was a tested and existing design and, what is more, could maintain flight on one engine in an emergency – a salient feature over huge jungle areas. Additionally, performance and bomb load characteristics for the BT-32 had been demonstrated and, with full tanks and 540 gallons of fuel, could loft 2,000 pounds of bombs some 1,000 miles – a fact which immediately gained the Colombian flag officer's attention. Curtiss-Wright was also equipping the BT-32 with controllable-pitch props, a relative novelty to the Colombians, but which managed to impress the General. Goulding, tossing specifications quickly, assured a maximum speed at 7,000 feet "well in excess of 170mph," with a cruising speed of 150mph and a ceiling of more than 23,000 feet.

Here, AM ground crews finish the mounting of four 116-pound bombs under the port wing of AM 651. The BT-32s were unquestionably the most potent bombers in Latin America as of 1934, and although the gun positions were faired over, the aircraft retained their bomber capability throughout their service lives.

The BT-32s were truly multipurpose aircraft. Besides mounting up to six 7mm defensive guns in two dorsal, two ventral, and two beam positions, they could mount a Fairchild F4 camera through a sliding door, had an Estoppey D-4 bomb sight, and could carry up to two 1,100-pound bombs and no fewer than 14 120-pound weapons in a combination of internal and underwing racks.

Historians who have been aware of this exchange have often wondered why, with the St. Louis factory essentially able to produce the BT-32s in fairly short order, they did not do so. The answer is simple: by the third week of April, 1934, there had been a concerted, nationwide series of strikes targeting aircraft manufacturing plants and, as a totally unexpected collateral effect, the workers at the Colt arms factory, where the multiple 7mm guns for the BT-32s were being built, honored the strikers by carrying out a work-slowdown.

Because of this, there was some discussion regarding the possibility of installing 37mm cannon in the BT-32s – like those which had been proposed for the Falcons – and Goulding instructed some of the Curtiss-Wright engineers to study that possibility; in the event, however, nothing came of it.

The BT-32s were all delivered as floatplanes via the Pan American base at Dinner Key, Miami, Florida and the Coco Solo Naval Air Station in the Panama Canal Zone, and then on to Barranquilla – certainly

The arrival of the first BT-32 at Barranquilla was an event, and it soon became apparent that handling the large aircraft on floats was going to require an entirely new protocol! The crews were striving to keep the BT-32 from drifting into the moored and camouflaged Falcon at right.

Before application of her serial number, AM 652 bears evidence, shortly after arrival, that she was to have been camouflaged, as her floats have already received the distinctive random scheme used on about half of the AM Curtiss aircraft. The ground crews give evidence of the scale of the aircraft.

among the largest biplanes to ever be mounted on floats – but complete sets of wheels were also delivered as well. Bearing Curtiss-Wright MSNs 54 to 56, they received AM serials 651 to 653.

The AM regarded these aircraft as bombers first and transports second, and they retained their bombardment capability throughout their service lives.

The three aircraft gave good service. AM 652 was lost November 15 or 17 (sources differ), when she was partially destroyed by fire while en route to Colombia's Atlantic coast with a load of mail and supplies for Colombia Army units, functioning as a floatplane at the time, and alighted on the Magdalena River. She was rated as 50 percent destroyed. She was apparently recovered and repaired, however, and was still in use – and counted as a bomber – on the September 28, 1945, Air Order of Battle!

AM 651 suffered damage on November 17 at Pinto and was a write-off, but 653 was the first to be lost entirely when she was destroyed by fire January 31, 1942, 16 miles southeast of Villavicencio in a bizarre incident. A German citizen, Dr. Hermann Steinmitz, confessed after the accident that he had intentionally set fire to the aircraft, causing her to make a forced-landing in the broad *llanos* on a return trip from Mito to Apiay. The pilot in command, Mayor Garcia Bonilla, was reportedly so incensed that he nearly shot the instigator after he had safely deplaned.

However, the AM was certainly not finished in its expansion. The tireless Colombian Consul in New York, Maximiliano Garavito, somehow became aware during the summer of 1934 that a solitary Consolidated (Fleet) Model 14 Husky, MSN 33, a rather well-used aircraft (having been built in 1929) had become available from Asbury W. Meadows of Buffalo, New York. The aircraft had been rather heavily modified, and in fact sported an Experimental Category License (X-524). It had a Gottingen

The BT-32s did not remain on floats for long. Here, 651 has had her gun blisters and glazed areas faired over and was being used as a pure transport. Note, however, that the bombs racks have been retained under the wings. This aircraft was lost on November 17, 1942, at Pinto.

398 airfoil and a Kinner K-5 engine, a cabin enclosure, and a larger-than-usual tail group – a truly hybrid aircraft.

Consul Garavito bought the aircraft, sight-unseen, on November 16, 1934, and advised the Civil Aviation Authority that it was to be shipped to Colombia around December 1, where it gained AM serial 48. The subsequent fate of this unusual aircraft is a complete mystery.

The AM had gained a healthy respect for the value of aircraft for communications, and for transport of men and equipment. Aircraft could invariably be pressed into service when necessary as armed auxiliaries, quite capable of patrols along the extensive river system of the country, especially, and in particular for keeping an eye on Peruvian movements and intentions.

The Junkers fleet, augmented by the BT-32s, gave the service one of the best, if not *the* best, air transport capabilities in Latin America at the time. However, the gradual attrition of existing assets by the fall of 1935 had led the Colombian Consul in New York to be instructed to search for even more aircraft capable of fulfilling this vital role.

It did not take him long to locate four secondhand Ford Tri-motors in the Chicago, Illinois, area, all of which, perhaps not coincidentally, were ex-Shell Oil Company aircraft, and he quickly snapped these up and financed modest refurbishment.

A bit of subterfuge may have surfaced at this point, as, when several of the aircraft were photographed at Floyd Bennett Field, they appeared to be wearing Ecuadorian national markings and simple, one-digit serial numbers, rather than the distinctive Colombian roundels. This may have been due to the U.S. Congressional investigation into the arms trade, which had caused Curtiss-Wright – and its customers – to be rather more prudent in their exchanges.

Initially, numbers simply 1 to 4 (numbers 1 and 3 on wheels, while 2 and 4 were mounted on huge Edo floats), the acquisition and overhaul process took longer than expected and the aircraft

Photos of Ford Tri-motors actually in service in Colombia are quite rare, but FAC 643, shown here in late 1930s-style national markings and rudder bands, even though of marginal quality, reveals the addition of a tall radio mast on the aft dorsal fuselage. This aircraft was lost on April 22, 1941, with a crew of five and nine passengers. It came down on the Brazilian side of the Puritú River while being flown by Capt. Jorge Bernal R.

The most forward permanent station of the AM during the conflict, the insignia of *Base Aérea Tres Esquinas* (originally *Puerto Boy*; it did not officially become *Tres Esquinas* until April 13, 1939), located at the confluence of the Putumayo and Orteguaza Rivers, lay some 300 miles south-southwest of Bogotá.

did not depart – after protracted diplomatic exchanges which appeared to show the U.S. State Department was stalling – until May 2–9, 1936. By June, following arrival, they had gained AM serials 641 to 644. These were Ford 5-AT-B MSN 5-AT-44, formerly NC-9687 (marked for delivery as "2"), and 5-AT-Cs MSN 5-AT-89 (ex-NC-429H), 5-AT-47 (ex-NC-9690, marked as "3" for delivery), and 5-AT-67 (formerly NC-408H). One of these, probably number "1," had been flown rather brazenly by Coronel Benjamin Mendez R. to the U.S. Army Air Corps' Bolling Field, DC, for the express purpose of meeting the Colombian Minister to the U.S., Dr. Miguel Lopez, and flying him and his wife home to Bogotá for the summer. Their rather leisurely trip through Mexico, Guatemala, El Salvador, and the relative luxury of USAAC facilities in the Panama Canal Zone, was viewed dimly by the State Department as nothing more than a high-pressure ploy to deflect the military nature of the aircraft. The other three aircraft were ferried to Colombia by the same Mayor Mendez and Capitáns Jose A. Estevez and Enrique Concha V.

The Fords, as everywhere, rendered spartan service to the AM, but three of them (by then FAC 642, 643, and 644) were written-off in accidents in 1941 alone. It appears that a fifth Ford, FAC 645, was acquired – possibly from SCADTA – as an aircraft with this serial was lost on January 30, 1943. The first aircraft, FAC 641, soldiered on as late as September 1945. Of the Colombian Fords, MSN 643 apparently saw the most extensive use, as by August 1941, after five years of service, it had amassed 531:10 hours in 505 flights. For the majority of their service lives, the Fords operated from Palanquero and Tres Esquinas.

Those Bellanca 77-140s

As noted previously, as early as 1933, Colombia had yearned for a dedicated, long-range heavy bomber – one which, true to their established procedure, could be operated on either wheels or floats. Curtiss-Wright was the first to respond to this requirement, but Colombian officials decided to hedge their bets by continuing a dialogue with the Bellanca firm of New Castle, Delaware, for what they expressed was a developed version of the Bellanca Airbus series.

This was the kind of aircraft that G. M. Bellanca could and did design, making use of as many of his tried-and-tested engineering concepts as possible – and which just happened to be the first aircraft he designed to mount two engines actually attached to the leading edges of the monoplane wing.

First emerging in 1934, the Model 77-140, with its powerful engines and lifting strut system, a Bellanca trademark, was ahead of its time in many respects. Even though designed against the Colombian specification, the order for the Curtiss-Wright BT-32s, for the time being, satisfied the AM. Bellanca, attempting to capitalize from the design effort, tried to market the design as the Bellanca Bimotored Transport, equipped with twin 715hp Wright Cyclones. The company had overtures for the bomber version from both Greece and Turkey but, as they both demanded an actual demonstration, Bellanca decided to hold out for an expected Colombian order.

Like other Bellanca designs, the odd designation was derived from the first two digits of the total wing area (770 square feet) and the first three digits of the combined horsepower of the two engines, rounded off to 700hp, or 1,400hp total. Sometimes cited in Department of State export documents as type 77-143, this may have been a more precise expression of the actual horsepower, 715hp, times two. For the record, the aircraft were described on the Bellanca Export License Application as "Bellanca Military Twin-Engined Heavy Duty, High Capacity Bomber Seaplanes"!

With a span of 76 feet (the wings could be folded) and, as a seaplane, standing some 20 feet, 6 inches tall, the aircraft could max out at 190mph as a landplane, and a respectable 175mph as a seaplane, with a ceiling of 28,000 and 22,000 feet, respectively. But more importantly, Bellanca guaranteed a range of 1,500 for either version – some 400 miles more than the BT-32s.

The aircraft was designed to be manned by a single pilot – a lot of airplane for one man – aided by a navigator/bombardier and two dedicated gunners. Bombs, totaling 2,825 pounds – slightly more than the BT-32s – were to be mounted on racks on the diagonal lower stub struts, between the wheels or floats of the undercarriage – and Bellanca informed the Colombians that provisions could also be incorporated for the aircraft to deliver "a torpedo or two."

Although enjoying a stout steel tube structure, it was fabric-covered in the interests of weight savings, and as a result, the interior was sparse and militarily utilitarian. It could be arranged, however, for use as a six-litter ambulance (as could the BT-32s), as a 12-place personnel transport or as an 18-place troop transport, although these soldiers would have had to know each other very well! There is evidence that a 180-gallon belly auxiliary fuel tank could also be fitted, increasing the range even more, but apparently the Colombian aircraft had only the 670-gallon internal tanks.

This unusual view of one of the Bellanca 77-140s reveals the folding-wing feature, the locations of the bomb racks under the lower-stub-wings, and the fact that the bombardier position windows were offset to starboard. The Edo floats were among the largest ever built.

The quartet of exotic Bellanca 77-140 bombers finally received by the AM in February 1935 are almost always illustrated wearing their huge Edo floats, but, in fact, at least one, AM 672, operated on a wheel undercarriage as late as July 1941. The insignia on the nose is that of *Base Aérea de Cali*.

The huge Edo floats were themselves 32 feet long but were not fitted to the first aircraft, which was tested in September 1934 on wheels – and at the same time, Bellanca made it known that he was working against a Colombian order for six of the aircraft.

By the end of 1934, Colombia had in fact placed an order, at $70,017 FAF, but for only four. The tireless Colombian Consul in New York hired U.S. pilots Virginius Clark and Herb Thaden to conduct a thorough inspection of the aircraft, and to make test flights of each. They, in turn, recommended certain changes, including a better fuel drainage system; some of the changes were made at Bellanca's expense, others at the expense of the customer.

The first two aircraft, MSN 1201 and 1203, were covered by Export License 3398 and were flight delivered to Cartagena, Colombia, in February 1935 – nearly a year later than planned. They flew down as seaplanes, with their bulky wheel undercarriages stowed in the fuselages. Each was flown down, in turn, by pilot Roger Q. Williams and co-pilot John L. Baker.

The first aircraft was forced down on the coast of Cuba because of a faulty oil line, and Williams complained that the aircraft had been completed too hastily at the time. But in fact, Bellanca certainly had more than enough time to get them right.

By May 18, 1935, all four of the aircraft on order had been completed, and the first two delivered. Sometime during 1936, however, one of the aircraft remaining in the U.S. had been flown to North Beach, Long Island, New York (where the Edo floats were installed), and was partially destroyed by a fire on May 10, 1936, started by careless smoking, burning the fabric off the entire right wing and from the cockpit to the tail. It is not clear if the Colombians were aware of this, as they were by this time bending every effort to cancel the entire order, claiming, among other things, that the first two, which had actually been delivered, were deficient in a number of unspecified respects – despite having accepted the go-ahead from their own hired examiners, noted above.

The first of the Bellanca 77-140 shortly after arriving on the flats near Cartagena. Sometimes described disparagingly as a "mass of spare parts flying in formation," the aircraft, although fearsome on paper, saw very limited use in Colombia.

The dispute on the remaining two aircraft – the two in Colombia were left idle while the dispute continued – were subject to a representation of the Spanish Republicans in August and September 1936 – and Bellanca, with the possibility of a $10,000 profit on the remaining two – was quietly informed by the State Department that a "moral embargo," for the moment, precluded them approving an export license for such a sale.

Finally, with his patience exhausted, and having made most of the changes to the remaining two aircraft at company expense, the last two 77-140s (MSNs 1202 and 1204) were finally delivered in September 1938, nearly four years after having been initially "completed."

In AM service, the aircraft were assigned serials 671 to 674, but a letter from the U.S. Military Attaché dated January 14, 1938, stated that the two on hand were still sitting idle as "the Colombian pilots are afraid to fly them." By July 1941, however, the aircraft had in fact been flown, as two were assigned to the base at Palanquero and two to Cali, and this was the final report making any mention of these unfortunate aircraft.

And Last but Not Least, Those Severskys

If Colombian exasperation had not been sufficiently tested by the sorry tale of the Bellanca 77-140s, the sage of the trio of Seversky SEV-3M-WW two-place, floatplane fighters surely must have done the trick.

As early as March 18, 1934, when the new SEV-3 could surely have been regarded as among the most advanced aircraft in the world, the Colombians rushed an order to the infant firm for no fewer than 18 of the aircraft while, at the same time, Seversky was enthusiastically demonstrating the aircraft to the Brazilian Army. These orders were facilitated, unfortunately, by none other than Alfred J. Miranda, Jr., of the American Armament Corporation, who eventually acquired an unsavory reputation.

One of the Seversky SEV-3M-WWs, AM 181, bearing the insignia of the *Base Aérea Cali*, which had been inspired by the American Volunteer Group. The aircraft were exceptionally maintenance intensive.

By late May 1934, a more modest order for six aircraft was noted, and this had been placed at precisely the same time as that for a mix of 12 Junkers types. Once again turning to well-known U.S. airmen to advise them on this acquisition, none other than Al Williams was engaged, and he apparently took his responsibilities very seriously indeed. He basically lived at the Seversky factory, overseeing every detail of the construction, and accompanied the company test pilot on every test flight (the aircraft had dual controls).

After completion, the three aircraft were flown to North Beach, Long Island (just like the Bellanca 77-140s), and, from there, shipped as deck cargo aboard the Japanese freighter *Nichi Maru* from Brooklyn to Colombia – accompanied all the way by Williams, his wife, and aviation engineer Warren G. Nichols.

Unloaded at Cartagena and assembled on the docks, Williams then very hastily oriented three of the most experienced AM pilots (who have escaped identification) and they were flown to Palanquero, some 600 miles up the Magdalena River. Williams, his wife, and Nichols then flew via SCADTA to Barranquilla, then on to Palanquero and finally Bogotá.

Initially, marked as simply "1" to "3" for test purposes, the aircraft were MSNs 1 to 3 (although 37 to 39 have also been suggested, for reasons that are not clear) and had also worn the Experimental Category Licenses X-15391, X-15689, and X-15928, respectively. They acquired AM serials 181 to 183.

On paper, the SEV-3M-WWs appeared to have potential. Equipped with 440hp Wright R-975E-3 engines, the manufacturer claimed a top speed of 260mph at 11,000 feet – and a respectable 220mph at sea level, in the realm where most AM activities would have been engaged. With flaps, they had a landing speed of 65–67mph, a bit hot for AM crews, and had a range, depending on configuration, of 700–900 miles.

The armament of the aircraft has always been the subject of some speculation, as none appears to have ever actually been fitted. However, they had provisions for two 7mm fixed Colt M-2s synchronized to fire over the nose, and a similar weapon for the guy in back – although it reportedly required considerable exertion to deploy in the tight compartment.

The Severskys were viewed with skepticism by even the most experienced AM pilots. With their amphibious wheels extended, as landplanes they were remarkably difficult to land, as pilots had trouble judging just how close to the flair they were. As a direct result of this, AM 183 was crashed at Madrid Air Base April 30, 1937, and both crew members were killed.

By October 16, 1937, the U.S. Attaché in Bogotá reported that the Colombians "do not like the Severskys, as they regard them as underpowered." The two survivors were dispatched to Cali and Palanquero, and the one at the latter station was reported as seldom flown. The one at Cali, however, was flown with apparent abandon by Captain J. L. Trunk, the Chief Instructor (noted earlier). Not to be outshone, the new AM Chief Instructor, Tte. Cabrera, decided to wring the aircraft out himself in similar fashion but, upon landing – his only one – he hit the ground with such force that the wheels were forced up through the floats, and the aircraft was badly damaged as a result, but repaired as a pure floatplane.

It did not take long for engineering aspects of the type to manifest themselves, in addition to the questionable undercarriage arrangement. Chief among these was the rather flimsy pyre line canopy cover, which very quickly suffered from the tropical heat and intense UV. It was also found to be extremely close-coupled for tall crewmen, who complained that in the super-heated, rough air of an afternoon, they were constantly impacting their heads with the canopy. As a direct result, at least one, AM 181, had the canopy removed altogether, retaining only the more robust windscreen, thus becoming one of the very few two-place, open-cockpit monoplane amphibian fighters!

By September 11, 1946, the two survivors were, remarkably, still on the Order of Battle, and were nominally assigned to the pursuit squadron at Palanquero, alongside 25 various North American AT-6s, three Falcons (two on wheels and one on floats), and eight Sea Hawks (four on wheels and the others on floats). They were not reported again.

The same aircraft late in her service life, minus the problematic pyrelene canopy. The pintle for the rear, flexible gun, can just be discerned aft of the crouching rear gunner. At the time they were introduced, even with their shortcomings, they were the most advanced aircraft in any Latin American air arm.

Chapter 7
Flying in Colombia

Most accounts of the Leticia period and the pioneering years of the AM and The Group's sojourn in Colombia have invariably focused on the hardware, limited action, and deployment. Little, on the other hand, has been provided to readers to aid in understanding what it was like to actually fly these exotic aircraft in what, for many, was the adventure of their lifetime.

A few firsthand accounts survive, including those of Jesse Rothrock, one of the principal pilots and officers of The Group. One of his earliest observations, often overlooked entirely by readers ignorant of the basic geography of Colombia, was that the capital, Bogotá, as of 1931–39, had no place to alight a seaplane; instead, the so-called "port" for the city at Girardot was used, located on the upper Magdalena.

He noted early on in his memoirs that

> we quickly learned that it was highly advisable to fly very early in the morning there, due to the heat, which blossomed very quickly. However, early mornings were also very often accompanied by dense fog over the rivers. This complicated flying along the upper part of the Magdalena, as there were several high mountain ranges that had to be crossed.

Some of those mountains, to the surprise of some of the Americans, were almost completely devoid of vegetation, and essentially appeared as immense rocks that quickly became heated by the nearly equatorial sun. This, in turn, heated the air around them, and caused the air to be, in Rothrock's vernacular of the time, "much less buoyant, and a plane had difficulty maintaining altitude."

He described the Magdalena as "winding its way through the mountains like a snake" and he noted a great number of rapids on the river. The preferred AM landing area on the river at Girardot constituted only a very short, straight stretch of the otherwise meandering river. You had to "come down between

Representing the most experienced members of the American Mission cadre, and two of whom are still wearing their U.S. wings, from left to right are Capitáns (assimilated) J. H. "Jesse" Rothrock (also known simply as "The Rock"), Ernest B. Nobile, and John Hayden. These instructors left a lasting imprint on the AM and the evolving FAC during their intensive 18-month tour of duty. Note the camera that Rothrock is holding, which took many of these images!

high cliffs (more than 200 feet) of rocky mountains – and then alight on a very narrow and swift flowing river." He noted that every landing there, especially to novice pilots, "gave a thrill, even when the weather was smooth."

Take-offs from Girardot were no less challenging. He said, "it is even harder, as the space is very limited by curves of the river and the high banks. Every take-off must be made by flying under the railway bridge, and crossing the river into the short straight-away."

While the instructors in The Group did the overwhelming majority of their training in dedicated training aircraft, they also had responsibility for gradually transitioning the cadets to the tactical types – first with wheels, and later, "for the very best students," onto float-equipped aircraft – usually a few PT-11Cs at first, then either Sea Hawks or Falcons. Ironically, by 1939, the AM had all but lost interest in float- and seaplane operations, aside from the few aircraft that retained floats or seaplane capability into the WWII years and, by 1945, the service had all but forsaken water-based flying.

One of the basic principles of flying into the Southern Zone, as has been alluded to earlier in this account, was the utter necessity of staying within sight of the principal waterway leading to the destination. There was very little flying over jungle terrain, unless by way of a well-known route. Although The Group made an effort to give instrument training on PT-11Cs, night flying was almost unheard of, and instrument flight, if practiced at all, was for flying in adverse weather, rather than nighttime.

In-flight views of aircraft during the Leticia emergency period are exceptionally rare. This Consolidated PT-11C is pictured over Cali on a typically stormy day, probably MSN 44.

Chapter 8
A Few Words About the Opposition

Recalling that this book is not intended to be a comprehensive study of the entire Leticia Affair but, rather, an effort to place the North American Mission and its contributions to the evolution of Colombian military aeronautics into perspective, it would be incomplete without a primer on the impetus behind it all – the potential of the *Cuerpo de Aeronáutica del Peru* (CAP).

Peruvian aviation historian and colleague Amaru Tincopa has published an excellent account of the war (*Air War Over the Putumayo*, published by Helion in their "Latin America@War" series, and now, unfortunately, out of print) written from the Peruvian perspective, and which may provide students of the subject and readers interested in the Peruvian political aspect, with additional details of the CAP involvement. But for the purposes of this narrative, at least a primer on "the opposition" is in order.

The Peruvian CAP had been born by the merger of Peruvian Army aviation (*Aviación Terrestre del Ejército*) and Peruvian naval aviation (*Servicio de Hidro-aviación de la Marina*) only a few short years prior to the incident in Leticia, on February 18, 1929 – one of the very first such mergers of national aviation energy anywhere. Following a bit of perhaps predictable confusion, the shotgun wedding of the two services was finally formally designed as the CAP on October 2, 1931.

Far better organized, structurally, then the substantially smaller Colombian air arm as of 1931, the leadership of the force wisely enabled the pre-merge training organizations, which had been dedicated respectively to land-based and water-based flying, to, for all intents and purposes, retain their previous character.

These were the Army's former *Escuela Central "Jorge Chavez"*, with two organic units (a primary training *4º Escadrille* and an advanced *5º Escadrille*) at Las Palmas Field, close to Lima, and the Navy's *Escuela de Hidro-aviación* at Ancón, on the Pacific coast to the west of Lima (where seaplane instruction was provided, also in primary and advanced stages, by the *7º Escadrille* and *2º Escadrille* respectively).

Yet another training unit, rather akin to an Operational Training Unit (OTU), the *3º Escadrille*, was located at distant Iquitos, some 650 difficult air miles north of Lima, not far from the confluence of the Amazon and Marañón and, of strategic importance to Peru, on the eastern side of the Andes and a scant 200 miles from Leticia – and even closer to the Putumayo.

The CAP also possessed two operational elements which Colombia had not as yet attained: the *1er Escuadrón de Reconocimiento* and a very experienced communications and transport element, the *1er Escuadrón de Transporte*.

With all of that, the amalgamated CAP was still, in reality, a service highly segregated by service identification, with long-serving naval officers and crews tending to look down on their Army comrades – a phenomenon found, however, in nearly every air arm on the planet, before and since!

Peru also had a substantial head-start on the Colombians in the realm of training and had, in effect, turned the training and leadership of their naval aviation element over to what amounted to an unofficial U.S. mission as early as January 1924.

Lieutenant Commander Harold B. Grow, U.S. Navy, was in fact designated as the Chief of Naval Aviation for Peru, and his stewardship, along with the small number of U.S. naval aviators and cadre that he assembled, had a profound impact on all that followed.

Adequately funded, by April 1924, Grow had been a ramrod. He had gotten a firm grip on the finances of the service and set about building proper barracks at Ancón for the enlisted ratings, separate CPO barracks, housing for officers – probably a first in Latin American aviation – an administration building, electric lights, an ice plant, a sewer system, water system, cement seawall, walks, gardens, machine shops, carpentry shops, blacksmith shops, test-stands, and fuel storage facilities. Ancón, in fact, took on the character of a U.S. naval air service, and was the envy of the Army aviators at Las Palmas and a model for Latin America as a whole.

However, more importantly, he set about acquiring U.S. aircraft types with which he was familiar, which turned out to be, perhaps not surprisingly, nearly all similar to those in line-service with the U.S. Navy.

Indeed, he reported to the Bureau of Aeronautics back in Washington that, when the first of the now nearly legendary Wright Whirlwind engines started to arrive from the U.S., the Peruvian crews "were like children opening Christmas presents, with exclamations of joy and pleasure as each new piece was taken out and carried carefully – like a precious package – into the hangars. It was the first time they had ever been given brand-new equipment to work with."

Grow's impact on the CAP, and its preparation for what the Peruvians came to call the "*Conflict del Nor-oriente,*" was profound – and, more to the point, benefited Peru long before the Colombians engaged the North American Mission.

True, Peru did not have the benefit of the SCADTA organization, infrastructure, and experienced personnel, but she did draw upon the equipment and bush-flying equipment of her own grassroots airline structure and, like Colombia, assimilated nearly all of these into the CAP Order of Battle.

Peru had also, at the recommendation of Commander Grow, started a Reserve Corps – initially of naval aviators – as early as 1925. He fundamentally sold the sitting government on the concept on the grounds that the relatively small Peruvian Naval Academy could not produce sufficient officer candidates for both aviation and fleet requirements – as well as nascent but growing civilian sector demands. The first six candidates for the Reserve commenced training in August 1925 and, by the time of the emergency, had accumulated considerable experience – at little cost to the service – while enhancing their own, personal portfolios. By mid-1929, the Army component of the air arm had finally started a similar system.

Equipping the CAP

As noted, the equipment choices made by the CAP were strongly influenced by recommendations made by Commander Grow and his staff, although some leftovers from desultory sales efforts of the 1920s by British, French, and U.S. interests flew on until they were essentially used up.

Primary instruction was carried on with the survivors of six Avro 504Ns acquired via an equipment-buying excursion made by none other than Coronel Juan Leguia to England in June 1927, where he purchased the aircraft on the spot for $50,000. These were supplemented by a maintenance-man's-nightmare of other types which had been acquired piecemeal. These included the survivors of five Boeing Model 21s, the first three of which had arrived in January 1925. Two were fitted out as floatplanes and the other as a landplane. By June 1926, despite one of these having been crashed as the result of a flat-spin (it was, remarkably, repaired and returned to flight status) the first three had accumulated more than 500 hours each. Essentially identical to U.S. Navy NB-1s, one was lost to a crash June 20, 1929, near Las Palmas, but the other four contributed significantly to the aerobatics training of the generation of CAP cadets that went to war with Colombia.

Among the aircraft used intensively to train the cadre of CAP pilots that went to war with Colombia were five examples of the Boeing Model 21, similar to the U.S. Navy's NB-1. Here, A-P 1-E-1 runs up at Ancón prior to a training sortie.

In addition to these aircraft, the training establishment also possessed single examples of the B.F.W. Flamingo (Udet U.12b, MSN 422), acquired in 1930 via the German Mission to the Peruvian Army which, remarkably, survived as late as February 1936, and a single Consolidated PT-3 Husky, MSN 6, which had been purchased directly from demonstration pilot Leigh Wade in 1928. Although wrecked several times, this aircraft also survived into early 1936.

The Air Pageant of September 23, 1932

Late in the same month as the incident at Leticia, and probably organized to demonstrate Peruvian aerial prowess to an aroused citizenry, the CAP conducted what was billed as an "Air Pageant" at Las Palmas, attended by the President of the Republic, the Minister of State, and representatives of the diplomatic and consular services, as well as a large crowd of citizens.

A fly-past was presented, which included a mix of six of the latest Vought Corsair variants acquired, "several" Travel Air Z4D trainers (although only one, coded E over TE-1G is known), the single examples of the Udet U.12b, the PT-3, and two Stearman C-3Rs. The CAP also managed to get one of the elderly Douglas DT-2B torpedo bombers into the air, and it flew in formation with a Bellanca CH, a de Havilland D.H.60 Moth and a Curtiss Oriole, as well as an assortment of Faucett aircraft which would shortly be seconded to the CAP, including two Stinson SM-1 Detroiters, two Travel Air A-6000s, a Panagra Ford Tri-motor, and two Fairchild FC-2s.

Described in U.S. intelligence reports as a Travel Air Z4D, this CAP trainer was highly regarded by the service for its rugged structure and excellent aerobatics characteristics. Here, E over TE-1G has been fitted out with a blind-flying hood, unusual at this juncture in a Latin American air service. The CAP apparently had at least two Z4Ds.

Although originally acquiring two examples each in December 1925 (MSN 253 and 254) and May 1927 (MSN 384 and 385), at least two mighty Douglas DT-2B torpedo bombers, including A-P 2-E-4 shown here as a trainer, remained in service by September 1932, and naval CAP crews were very experienced on the type.

Chapter 9
Opening Moves and the Combat Period

Although the CAP seemed to appear to hold a quantitative and experience advantage over the Colombians, the Peruvians were operating over challenging distances, and the logistics requirements of maintaining its fighting force at the distant Iquitos staging base were daunting. This resulted in an urgent requirement for dedicated transport aircraft to shuttle parts, ammunition, lubricants, and crews from the far rear. Thus was formed what was cited at the time as the *Linea a la Montaña*, a quasi-airline operating between Las Palmas and Iquitos, starting around October 24, 1932. Their initial equipment consisted of a former Panagra Fairchild Model 71 (FC-2W2), MSN 532 (NC-9715), joined in April 1933 by another, MSN 629 (NC-9116) via Harold Grow. These and the other aircraft used on this line apparently had single-digit numbers painted on their fins to denote their identities, the former having gained number "8."

The sturdy Fairchilds joined two equally stout Hamilton H-45s, MSN 43 and 44 (formerly C-5562 and NC-5832) acquired in May 1930, and which had been coded outright as CAP aircraft, becoming 1-R-10 and T-051, the former, oddly, being a tactical code for a reconnaissance aircraft. The hard-working Hamiltons joined three brand-new Boeing Model 40B-4s (MSNs 1160 to 1162), which had been delivered from Seattle starting in late March 1930.

But the pointy end of the CAP, which had been pre-positioned at Iquitos even before the so-called "spontaneous" invasion at Leticia, consisted of a mix of Vought O2U-1E Corsairs, all mounted on floats, which the CAP had started receiving as recently as mid-July 1930, totaling a mix of some ten aircraft. The CAP started moving these armed aircraft to the appropriately designated *Escuadrón de Reconocimiento*[1] as early as October 5, 1932 (the first three), followed by one more on November 8, another two on Christmas day, and a final example April 22, 1933. They were first shipped on trains to Jauja, where they were mounted on wheels, then flown to San Ramón and then on to Sotziki, where floats were installed under primitive field conditions. Finally, with the floats fitted, they flew on – most for the very first time – from there to Masisea, after taking off from the Perené River and then, finally, to Iquitos. The first aircraft to complete this very demanding trek was 5-E-1, flown by Tte. Francisco Secada Vigneta and 5-E-6 flown by Cpt. Leonardo Alvariño Herr.

Two others, for a total of nine aircraft, had crashed en route, one on February 20, 1933, and one on March 11, 1933. Ironically, these aircraft – apparently all O2U-1Es – retained their "trainer" codes and included 2-E-1 to 2-E-5 as well as 5-E-1, 5-E-2, and 5-E-6. This constituted nearly all of the O2U-1Es on hand with the CAP, as one had been lost in Huaraz at the hands of revolutionary forces before the Leticia emergency and another at Las Palmas on purely training duties on January 13, 1931. The seldom-mentioned O2U-3Bs, much more modern versions of the same basic design – which almost certainly were exported by the United Aircraft Export Corporation as some variant of the V.65 or V.66 series – did not arrive in-country until 1933.

The CAP appeared to enjoy a margin on superiority, at least on paper – but this didn't last long. The first CAP missions consisted essentially of regional familiarization flights, as not a single one of the pilots had ever flown in this sort of terrain or under these very tropical conditions.

What is more, the CAP detachment in the area of conflict had only the most fragmentary information about what they might encounter in terms of Colombian opposition and, reportedly, there were rumors that the opposition might include veteran combat aviators of the German Air Service of WWI which was, at least in part, correct.

Back in Lima, the CAP leadership had finally become aware of the extent of Colombia's expansion of her own air arm and managed to mobilize an effort and the financing to match what they had learned. One of the very first major expenditures, and the importance of which has been all but overlooked, was for $45,000 worth of Pratt & Whitney Wasp engines and spare parts to repair many of those already on hand. The Wasp series was the very backbone of the entire service.

By February 1933, the Curtiss-Wright Export Corporation, rather shamelessly stoking the fires in the midst of a do-or-die depression environment, had enlisted the services of none other than Elmer J. "Slim" Faucett, a legend in his own time, to be the point man for their ambitions in Lima.

The campaign to sell aircraft to Peru started innocently enough. Faucett had made arrangements to bring a Canadian-built Curtiss-Reid Rambler sesquiplane demonstrator into Peru from Chile – but learned that the Peruvian government was demanding a 5 percent duty on the declared value of the aircraft ($3,000), and that the duty be paid in Chilean *pesos* at an exchange rate of 45 *pesos* to the dollar.

As it turned out, Faucett told Curtiss-Wright that the duty mentioned was "the bootleg rate-of-exchange – the official government rate was actually 16.50 *pesos* to the dollar." C. W. Webster, the sparkplug behind the Curtiss sales drive of the time, also advised Faucett to tell the government that the "Rambler does not belong to you but is the property of the Curtiss-Wright Export Corporation of New York. This is for the purpose of preventing any possibility of confiscation during the period of the government's little comic-opera war!"

By this time, Webster and his front-men had closed a deal with the CAP for three Curtiss Model 35-A Sea Hawk Type Is (MSNs SH-7/11671 to SH-9/11673) – identical in every respect to those they were shipping to Colombia at precisely the same moment. He had advised Faucett that the new aircraft would probably be assembled at Las Palmas, rather than at Ancón, and that the twin-floats on which they were to be mounted would be shipped upriver, in a pattern similar to the delivery of the O2U-1Es. Webster also rather pointedly asked Faucett if there was any possibility of selling additional Sea Hawks to the CAP, hinting that the number going to Colombia was much larger.

The CAP made a rather short-sighted decision when they acquired the trio of Sea Hawks, however. They did not order any spare engines, or extra parts, oversights which would come back to haunt them in the days ahead.

By March 15, 1933, as events in the combat zone were starting to warm up, J. V. Van Wagner, representing Curtiss-Wright Export in Santiago, Chile, wrote to Webster advising that the Peruvian ambassador there wanted "immediate action" with regard to the delivery of single examples of a Curtiss D-12 powered Hawk and Falcon, which the company had maintained there as demonstrators. The payment for these otherwise exotic aircraft – which would be the only D-12 powered aircraft in Peru – was deposited in the Chase National Bank in New York and came to a tidy $36,000.

The problem was getting the aircraft out of Chile and flown to Peru. At first, they attempted to dismantle them and ship them to Peru via surface vessel but, in the event, with the application of discretionary funds into the right hands, by March 30 they had been cleared to leave Chile and fly to Peru, the facilitator being a man named Orsini, although the home office begged its agents in the field to always cite him as "Mr. Jones"! As it turned out, the D-12 powered aircraft acquired via Chile included a second Falcon, and it is assumed that this is one that was diverted from those being assembled near Santiago at the so-called Curtiss "factory."

While Curtiss-Wright was attempting to close deals with the CAP, they learned in late March 1933 that the Peruvians had concluded an aircraft order with French interests, totaling credit for 23–35 million *francs* (about $1,400,000 at the rate of exchange at that time) and this included an array of training and operational aircraft, as well as armament, radios, camera equipment, and spares. The Peruvian government had agreed to pay 700,000 *francs* per month on this order, but demanded delivery be completed in eight months.

Curtiss-Wright, probably correctly, stated that there was no possible way they would agree to such terms, as they suspected that, after the equipment had actually been delivered after eight months, the French would be stuck with an unpaid balance when the emergency subsided. They also pointed out that United Aircraft Export Corp., which had delivered the Vought aircraft to the CAP, was, as of March 1933, "still holding the bag for about $700,000." The French deal, as reported to Curtiss-Wright, was to consist of a mix of 12 Breguet Bre-27s, 12 Potez 390A.2s, and an equal number of Morane-Saulnier MS-231s, which were being rather generously described as "multi-purpose machines," when in fact they were, at best, basic trainers.

Then, out of nowhere, Curtiss-Wright learned that the CAP had somehow managed to place an order with Douglas for six O-38Ps,[2] closed on October 17, 1932, and that the company had actually promised delivery by January 1933! This strongly suggests that these aircraft had already been laid down for another customer (probably China) as, indeed, the six aircraft arrived aboard the S.S. *Ucayali* at Callao, where they were quickly conveyed to Las Palmas for assembly. These aircraft, armed with but two 7.65mm guns (one synchronized, fixed and one flexible, with A-3 bomb racks under each wing) formed the equipment of a second combat unit, the *2º Escadrille de Reconocimiento* of the *1º Escuadrón Aérea*. Coded 1/2-VG-1 to 1/2-VG-6, three of these (-2, -4, and -5) were, after rather perfunctory crew familiarization, dispatched via Bayóvar to Santa María de Nieva and Itaya to the Amazon region, converting to twin-floats en route.

Sometimes cited in intelligence documents of the day as O-38Ss, as noted earlier, the performance of these aircraft wasn't quite what the CAP had hoped, and they soon resorted to removing the engine speed rings in the zone of operations due to persistent overheating experienced by the 640hp Wright Cyclone engines. This sudden shift from the ambitious and well-financed Curtiss-Wright machine came as a shock, but as the CAP quickly learned, quick delivery wasn't necessarily a panacea. They soon switched their allegiances back to Curtiss-Wright and Vought due not only to operational considerations, but to the strength of a *guano* contract that a Mr. Love had only recently negotiated, and very generous credit extended by the United Aircraft Export Corporation, representing Vought.

The CAP attempted to squelch adverse reports trickling in from the Amazon from combat crews who reported that the O-38Ps were no match for the AM Sea Hawks they were encountering which, unbeknownst to the CAP, were operating on 87 octane aviation fuel, which was not available in Peru.

By the end of April 1933, after a scant three months of operations, only three of the O-38Ps remained. One was lost on its ferry flight somewhere between Paita and Iquitos, and two others were completely washed out at Iquitos, well behind the lines, costing the life of one very experienced aviator.

Besides the imports, the CAP, like Colombia, also hastened to identify and acquire aircraft for the cause already in the country. They essentially commandeered a Panagra Fairchild 2W2 (Model 71), MSN 532 (the former NC-9715) and shipped it by rail to Jauja, where she was assembled and flown on to San Ramon, where it was hastily applied with national markings and used, to good effect, to transport men and munitions between San Ramon and Masisea. One Panagra staff member claimed it was simply seized, while another characterized it as a "patriotic loan."

The only four-gun fighter of the Leticia conflict, the three CAP Vought V-80Ps arrived too late to influence the fighting – leaving Peru as the solitary operator of the type.

The Fairchild 71 was soon joined by a Faucett Travel Air cabin monoplane, probably a 6000-series aircraft, for which the company was paid $7,000. It, too, was immediately flown to San Ramon and pressed into service.

The final acquisition made by the CAP during the closing stages of open conflict consisted of three truly exotic Vought V-80P single-seat fighters, MSNs 992 to 994, coded initially as III over 2-C-1E to 2-C-3E. Fitted with Pratt & Whitney T1C1 Hornets rated at 700hp, these were the only four-gun fighters acquired during the conflict, with two synchronized to fire through the prop and two others in the upper wing. They also sported, as usual, A-3 bomb racks under the lower wings, and claimed a maximum speed in excess of 190mph. They were viewed as the CAP's answer to the AM's Model 65 Sea Hawk IIs. But, like so many of the aircraft acquired by both sides during the emergency, they arrived far too late to influence the outcome.

Peru, like Colombia, in addition to the efforts noted to this time, then also set off on an aircraft buying spree, acquiring significant numbers of additional aircraft from the U.S., Britain, France, and, of course, somewhat later, Italy. But those buys have been described in detail in other works by this writer and others and exceed our remit in this narrative.

By September 9, 1935, after the crisis had, for the most part, passed, the CAP had all but stood down, and nearly all of its tactical aircraft had been augmented by the first of the mass infusion of Italian types. The disposition of the service in the following snapshot as of that date is illuminating, in that it reveals aircraft acquired during the Leticia period, and suggests losses to known acquisitions during the course of the conflict. These were manned, after the mobilization, by some 600 officers, 400 enlisted ranks who were regarded as aircrew, 300 conscripts, and 52 cadets in training.

At the Central Flying School, *Escuadrilla de Instrucción*, Las Palmas
Morane-Saulnier M.S.110 = 5 (of 6 acquired)
Hanriot H-438 = 5 (of 12 acquired)
Potez 390A.2 = 2 (of 15 acquired)
Caproni Ca 113 = 1
Caproni Ca 114 = 3
Curtiss D12 Falcon = 2
Vought O2U-1E Corsair = 1

Escuadrón No. 1 (Bombardeo) Las Palmas
Caproni Ca 114 = 6
Caproni Ca 111 = 6
Stearman C-3R = 1

Escuadrón No. 4 Chiclayo
Curtiss Cyclone Falcon = 6
Curtiss 35-A Hawk Type I = 6

In Storage at the *Maestranza Central*, Callao and the *Estación Hidro-aviación*, Ancón
Potez 390A.2 = 9
Caproni Ca 114 = 2
Nieuport-Delage NiD-121C.1 = 11
Fairey Fox = 4
Fairey Gordon = 5
Caproni Ca 111 = 5
Vought V.80P = 2
Morane-Saulnier M.S.231 = 1
Ford 4-AT Tri-motor = 1

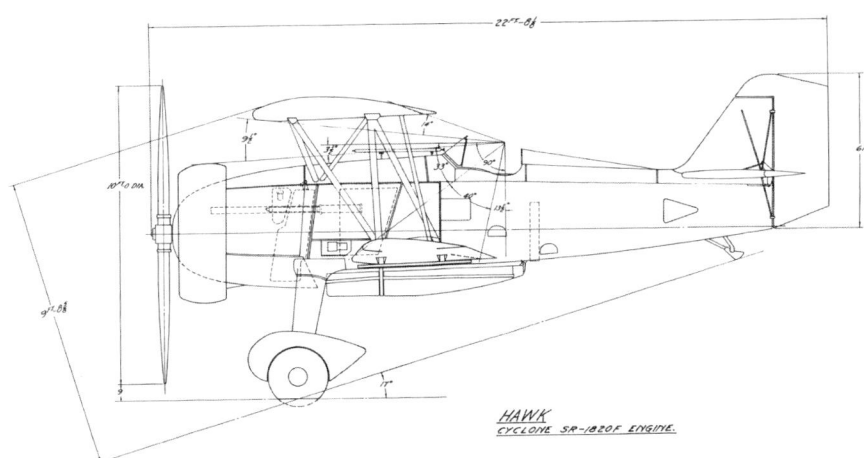

Colombia ultimately acquired three separate variants of the classic Curtiss Hawk, the designations for which have been very misunderstood since the 1930s: the Type 35-A Sea Hawk Type I which, despite its name, could be flown on wheels or twin floats; the Type 65 Sea Hawk II; and a single Type 65-A Hawk II-A. This Curtiss-originated line drawing shows the SR-1820F-powered Hawk II. (Curtiss)

Epilogue

And so, America's first Volunteer Group, the members of which had almost certainly entertained thoughts of adventure and even glory as they sailed into the tropics, faded into obscurity, having left behind a training establishment which the AM, subsequently renamed as the *Fuerza Aérea Nacionales* (FAN) and later, *Colombiana* (FAC), adopted as its own, with but scant memory of those halcyon years when the force suddenly matured into a world-class air force.

There are a number of questions that remain unanswered regarding the aviation component of this little-known conflict. Perhaps the most glaring of these revolve around the curious mix of American and German equipment, most of which, acquired new, were state-of-the-art as of 1931–34.

Above left: With their accumulated pay, the members of The Group were able to enjoy hand-tailored suits and exotic off-duty pursuits. Here, Addison, one of the instructors, poses at Cali with a mysterious Stinson SM-1 *Detroiter* just visible in the right background. It is unclear what it was doing at a strictly military airfield.

Above right: Known universally within The Group as "Pop," this older pilot soon discovered that handling the administrative duties of the organization was less stressful than screaming at Colombian cadets. The aircraft behind him appears to be one of the PT-11Cs.

Curtiss-Wright clearly dominated the scene, and only rather half-hearted efforts have been documented suggesting that other U.S. manufacturers, equally hungry during the depths of the Depression, made any effort at all to sell aircraft to Colombia. Vought, via the United Aircraft Export Corp. and their representative in Colombia, Manuel Toro, offered six variants of their V.65 Corsair series and had supplied Toro with a selection of catalogs and performance data, but Douglas, Boeing, and Waco – the latter of which was certainly well poised to supply float-equipped JHD and WHD light combat types – appear to have remained strangely quiet through it all.

Ironically, one other U.S. manufacturer of the period made overtures for AM business as early as February 16, 1933. Lockheed, of Burbank, California, had sent the U.S. Embassy staff literature on their Orion and Vega series, implying that, besides being fully capable of being operated on floats, these could be "easily armed for use as combat planes."

And one other very unlikely contender also stepped up. The Monocoupe Corporation, which had sold a single Model 90Js and three model 110/6Ws to the *Escuela de Aviación Civil* managed by Ernesto Samper, had sent salesman Scotty Burmood to Colombia to attempt to sell additional aircraft to the AM, although precisely how they would have contributed to the emergency remains unclear. A vague reference to them being adaptable for training (the crew sat side by side) seems unlikely, but their use as "dispatch" aircraft, with their relatively short range, would have restricted use to airfields along the coast and Palanquero, and not in the combat zone. Burmood had in fact flown one of the 110/6Ws, painted bright yellow, over the city during Zornosa's funeral cortege. He was disdainful of the students of the EAC, however, reportedly stating that "not a single one of the 15 students at the school had any real knack for flying, and that it just was not in their blood." He did not endear himself to audiences to whom he was attempting to sell airplanes.

His rather condescending view of the school's students was, unfortunately, reinforced in early April 1933, when two of them stole – and then wrecked – the best of the Model 110/6Ws. Exactly where they intended to go with the aircraft remains unclear. The family of one of the boys, suffering acute embarrassment,

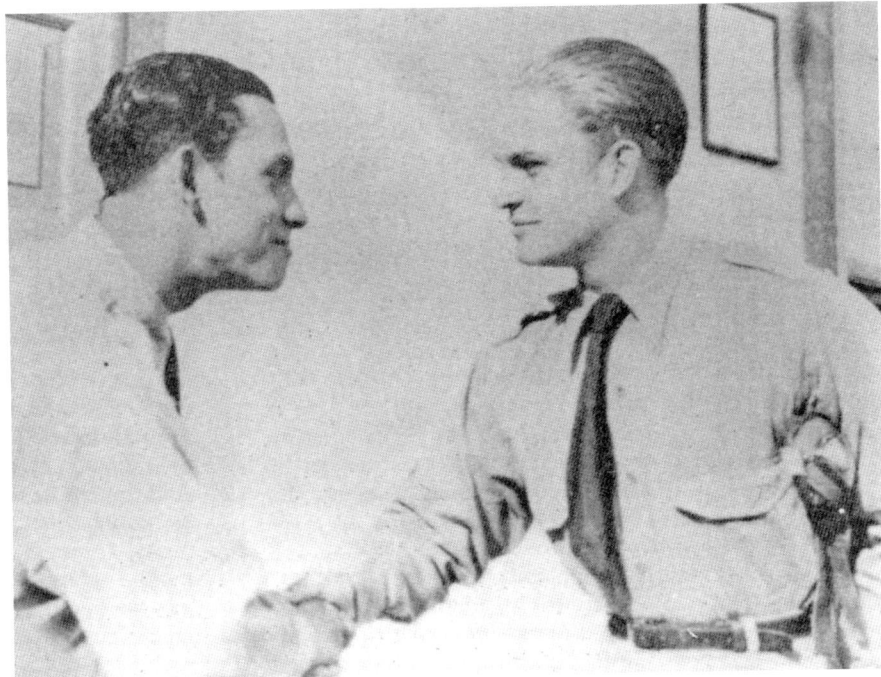

An entire generation of Colombian military cadets were trained by the American Mission cadre, including Antonio Calle (left) and Alberto Pauwels, pictured here at graduation at *El Guabito*, Cali, in 1936. Many went on to flag rank in the FAC. The PT-11Cs could also be mounted on twin Edo floats.

Colombia acquired 18 sturdy Consolidated PT-11Cs starting in March 1934, numbered 30 to 47 (MSNs 37 to 54). Here, MSN 32 is seen in flight being flown by Sub Teniente Antonio Calle, who had a date with destiny with the same aircraft that very day.

Unfortunately, Consolidated PT-11C MSN 32 broke up in-flight during exuberant aerial maneuvers while being flown by freshly minted Sub Teniente Antonio Calle over Cali August 23, 1938. Here, the upper main plane departed from the aircraft and crashed into an electrical pole just next to the base headquarters building.

The shattered remains of PT-11C MSN 32, which lost her main upper wing and rudder over Cali, leading to the death of one of the most promising of the cadets trained by the American Mission. Oddly, a postwar Air Order of Battle still showed MSN 32 on strength as of February 5, 1943, suggesting that the aircraft was somehow, miraculously, rebuilt.

actually paid for a replacement. Samper, somewhat buoyed by the outcome, then departed for the U.S. with Burmood with additional funds from the Ministry of Industry and some of his own to buy three more.

British and Dutch aircraft figured in the equation only to the extent that they were engaged as bargaining chips to secure better terms from Curtiss-Wright, while the French, essentially still embarrassed by their last mission to Colombia, enjoyed success in Peru but not a whimper in Colombia. However, as of April 15, 1933, Potez and Nieuport-Delage were attempting to sell a mix of 20 aircraft to Colombia directly – and, like Curtiss, apparently felt little compunction to inform the AM that they were selling essentially the same types to the Peruvians.

Ironically, one of the offspring of the entire episode was a short-lived AM aerobatics team, mounted on seven of the nimble wheel-equipped Sea Hawks, known as the *Escuadrilla de la Aurora*, established at Cali in 1937 – the first known dedicated aerial demonstration team in Latin America. Their pilots flew with a new discipline and pride, and many of them eventually rose to positions of power and influence in the course of their service to their homeland.

The insignia for *Base Aérea Cali* located in southwest Colombia, about 190 air miles from Bogotá.

Endnotes

Chapter 2: The *Aviación Militar* at the Dawn of the 1930s
1. Throughout this book, the title of the service during this entire period is abbreviated as AM. The service did not become the *Fuerza Aérea Nacional* until July 15, 1942, and was not officially renamed as the present-day *Fuerza Aérea Colombiana* until December 31, 1944.
2. Mendez had learned to fly in 1924 at the Curtiss school at Garden City, Long Island, New York, on Curtiss JN-4Ds, and had been issued FAI License No. 6184 on September 16, 1924.
3. Colombia was so anxious to obtain such utilitarian aircraft that, on September 3, 1932, it had requested that two U.S. Army Air Corps Loening OA-1As, then on strength with the 19th Composite Wing in the nearby Panama Canal Zone, be immediately sold to them "in order to maintain order within Colombian territory on the Peruvian border."
4. General Antonio Ricaurte who, in the campaign of Simon Bolivar for the liberation of South America from Spanish rule, is reputed to have fired a pistol into a barrel of gun powder in a munitions depot during the battle for Junin in Venezuela. The depot was Bolivar's last resource in the bitter fighting, and Ricaurte waited until hundreds of Spanish troops and officers were inside the depot, destroying it and claiming his own life in the process. Ricaurte's image is the symbol of the modern-day Colombian Air Force and the name of its highest decoration.
5. The K 43 could potentially be fitted with two dorsal gun positions, although the AM trio apparently had provisions for only one, for either single or twin gun mounts, as well as the ventral door gun. In addition, one or two fixed, forward-firing guns could be installed, but Junkers actually advised potential customers against this installation.

Chapter 3: The Curtiss-Wright Connection
1. Samper was the son-in-law of Dr. Carlos A. Urueta, which may explain much. According to a U.S. intelligence document dated April 7, 1931, contracts for aircraft bids were not "open" to public bid, and those of Curtiss-Wright Export were invariably the highest received! Samper was ably aided in all of this by George Chapline, who arrived at Barranquilla on the S.S. *Colombia* on March 16, 1933. He was none other than the Director of Sales and Service for Curtiss-Wright Export Corp.
2. As early as December 20, 1933, the AM had asked Curtiss-Wright Export Corp. for a quote on 31 Sea Hawks, 30 Falcons, and 12 Condor IIs.
3. On January 25, 1934, the AM advised Consolidated that they desired to acquire no fewer than 11 more P2Y-1Cs! Interestingly, the AM placed an order with Consolidated on March 27, 1935, for 24 specialized blueprints for the P2Y-1C type, which included complete sets for the pilot's enclosure, the hull structure assembly, and wing installation, suggesting that they were in the midst of rebuilding an aircraft. The drawings were to be shipped to Buenaventura.

Chapter 4: Colombia Attacks
1. This force has been variously described but probably consisted of one of the new Junkers K 43s, the two newest Dornier Do J Wal IIds, a former SCADTA Junkers F 13 that had been armed in some fashion, and three of the earliest Curtiss Model 35-A Sea Hawk Type Is, all float-equipped.

2. These aircraft included one of the new Junkers K.43s, two of the camouflaged Dornier Wals, one of the ex-SCADTA Junkers F 13s, and three of the brand-new Curtiss 35-A Sea Hawk Type Is.
3. The majority of these were apparently Model 35-A Sea Hawks, one of which reportedly sustained some 28 bullet holes in its airframe during the engagement.
4. The spelling of the name of this remote village has been variously reported, also being cited as Gueppi.
5. The captain died of his wounds two weeks later. Brazil registered no protest against the attack, as they soon realized that the vessel had been in the service of Colombia and was thus a valid target, although it is not clear if the attacking aircraft knew this at the time.
6. The aircraft crashed May 22 on the Putumayo near Caucayá and the crew consisted of Tte. Herbert (also given as Heliberto) Gil, Cpt. Haennichen (German), and three others on board, described as mechanics Narciso Combariza, Rafael Fernandez (both Colombians), and Erik Rettich (German), the sole survivor. Based on the description of the loss, the aircraft was apparently overloaded. Only one of the crew members was recovered. Rumors circulated for some time that the aircraft had actually been shot down by a Peruvian aircraft, but this cannot be substantiated.
7. The fact that many Germans had legally immigrated to Colombia after WWI and become Colombian citizens has clouded the identities of many of these aviators for years. As of May 1933, AM pilots who were Colombian citizens consisted of the following:

    Mayor Benjamín Méndez Rey
    Mayor Eduardo Gómez Posada
    Capitán Camilo Daza
    Capitán Andrés M. Díaz
    Capitán Luis F. Gómez Niño
    Capitán Arturo Lema Posada
    Capitán José A. Cabrera
    Capitán Abraham Liévano
    Capitán Jorge Méndez Calvo
    Capitán Enrique Santamaria M.
    Capitán Ernesto Esguerra
    Capitán José Estéves
    Capitán Alfredo Duarte
    Tte. Eduardo Escandón
    Tte. José Ignacio Forero
    Tte. Hernando García
    Tte. Aurelio Gutiérrez
    Tte. José J. Obando
    Tte. Uladislao O'Byrne
    Tte. Francisco Santos
    Tte. Enrique Concha

Pilots who flew during the early stages of the conflict who were German citizens included the following. Their ranks cited here, other than that of Herbert Boy, may have been assimilated AM ranks, or their status as previously established while in the employ of SCADTA:

    Coronel Herbert Boy
    Capt. Olaf Bielenstein
    Capt. Mauren Brecker

Capt. Fritz Von Donop
Capt. Ferrucio Guicciardi
Capt. F. Tesseas Von Heydebreck
Capt. Hans Kinderman
Capt. Karl Maringer
Capt. Alexander Mauke
Capt. Von Oertzen
Capt. Johan Ristiez
Capt. Rudolf Starke
Capt. Hans Wermer von Engel
Capt. Ludwig Graf-Schaesberg
Capt. Henry Grautoff
Capt. Hans Dietrich Hoffmann
Tte. Helmuth Koening

Observer/gunners of German citizenship known to have flown during the conflict included:
Sub.Tte. Adolf Edler Von Graere
Sub.Tte. Bodo Von Kaull
Sub.Tte. Paul Mutter
Sub.Tte. Hans Himpe
Sub.Tte. Heinz Kutscha

Chapter 5: Curtiss-Wright Arrives in Force, Just as the Dust Settles

1. By April 15, 1933, the Colombians, having learned that Curtiss was selling these aircraft to Peru as well, sent an urgent cable to Curtiss demanding to know under what terms they would be willing to sell only to Colombia!
2. These were FAC serials 801a, 803 to 805, 808 to 811, 813 and 814, 817, 819, 821 and 822, 824 and 825. Of these, all but four (813, 817, 819, and 821) had returned to wheel undercarriages.
3. The story goes that most of these officers, who had been implicated in a revolutionary attempt in their homeland and held as political prisoners, were released to serve in Colombia as a convenient way to salve local sensitivities and get them out of the country at the same time. They included Eduardo Laborde, Mario Forest, Manuel Ferro Mantoto, and Aurelio Ruiba.
4. This MSN has also been attributed to a single ex-SCADTA Dornier Do B Merkur I, but not a single shred of documentary evidence or photographic corroboration has been located. In any case, it would have been "out of sequence" and conflicted with the known Wal acquisitions.

Chapter 6: *El Misión de Aviación Norteamericana*

1. Jesse Rothrock, one of the leaders of The Group, stated in a letter dated January 6, 1970, to this author that, originally, The Group had been hired, undoubtedly, to "fight the Peruvians."
2. A complete list of all of the members of The Group has never been found. Colombian sources identify The Group rather differently, listing 24 pilots, 29 mechanics and technicians, and 14 wives, all arriving at Cartagena. Their personal baggage consisted of 300 steamer trunks and 180 suitcases! Those who have been identified, besides those already mentioned, included:
    Carl E. Chido
    George H. Pickenpack

Paul Herman
Sam LoPresti
"Baldy" Terrell
Mulligan
Kelly
Patterson
Addison
Henry Vaughan
Starke
McLeod
Bush
Chappel
Peenstra
John H. Hayden (and wife "Billie")
"Pop" Curran
Bubeck
Haley
Woodward
Lundy
Lasche
John L. "Sunny" Trunk
Olink (also given as Olin) Haley
Ernest (also given as Easton) B. Nobile (also given as Nobley!)
Gordon W. Silva – mechanic
Todd Hunter – accompanied Mendez in the Curtiss D-12 Falcon, *Ricaurte*, and, by April 1933, had been actively engaged in the combat zone as the solitary qualified mechanic on the Model 35-A Sea Hawks. He reportedly had also been flying transports (possibly including the solitary Hamilton H45/47) and had been present during the battles at Tarapaca and Güepi.
William J. Crosswell – the Curtiss-Wright test pilot at Palanquero
Oscar W. Carlson (killed in an accident near Madrid Air Base, Cundinamarca)

3. On March 6, 1934, Curtiss-Wright had submitted a detailed request through the new Roosevelt Reconstruction Finance Corporation (RFC) to fund the financing of a further 18 Sea Hawks, 18 Falcons, and 12 Condor IIs, including the cash purchase of six Sea Hawks, six Falcons, and three Condor IIs "recently" at a total price tag of $2.3 million. Two-fifths of the cost, they suggested, would be met during that current year and that $560,000 was necessary to pay for 15 aircraft already bought, which was to be remitted by Colombia's bank by May, together with an additional $190,000. Starting August 1, 1934, further payments of $50,000 per month would be made by the bank of the Republic to Curtiss-Wright until the end of the year, totaling $1 million for 1934. The problem confronting Curtiss-Wright was securing the other $1.5M. The Colombian government, naturally, wanted credit, but Curtiss-Wright, in the midst of the Depression and nearly on its last legs, could not finance all of this. Curtiss-Wright was thus asking for the financing of this huge order by the RFC.

4. It is interesting to note that, between 1931 and November 16, 1932, Trunk was the registered owner of a Curtiss Fledgling, NC-483K (MSN B-87) domiciled at Valley Stream, NY, on Long Island. The aircraft was cancelled without stated reason and may well have gone to Colombia although the

Fledgling J-2s the AM acquired were all believed to have been newbuild aircraft. He had also gained slight press coverage, rather obliquely, on September 1, 1929, when, on a "test flight" as instructor with none other than aviatrix Fay Gillis, the tail of their Curtiss Fledgling suddenly separated from the aircraft and both took to their Irvin parachutes. Gillis thus became the very first woman to become a member of the exclusive Caterpillar Club! She was wearing a skirt at the time, which must have made for an interesting descent.

Chapter 9: Opening Moves and the Combat Period

1. Apparently, this unit was redesignated as the *1º Escuadrón Aérea* shortly after the arrival of the O2U-1Es, commanded by Tte. Cdr. Baltazar Montoya.
2. Oddly, U.S. intelligence reports and even U.S. Commercial Attaché reports, as early as April 1933, invariably cited these aircraft as type O-38S, and claimed that they were rather hurriedly funded by the *Colecta Nacional*.